World's Greatest Mint Errors

A Guide to the Most Spectacular
Major Mint Error Coins

By Mike Byers

The publisher and editor of minterrornews.com
and Mint Error News Magazine

Edited by: Jeff Ambio

World's Greatest Mint Errors

A Guide to the Most Spectacular
Major Mint Error Coins

By: Mike Byers

Edited by: Jeff Ambio

Coin Images and Selected Text Copyright © 2009 Mike Byers or *minterrornews.com*
Coin Descriptions and Selected Text Copyright © 2009 Zyrus Press

Published by:
Zyrus Press Inc.
PO Box 17810, Irvine, CA 92623
Tel: (888) 622-7823 / Fax: (800) 215-9694
www.zyruspress.com
ISBN-13: 978-1-933990-02-6 (hardcover)
ISBN-10: 1-933990-02-3
Printed in China

Cover Design and Layout © 2009, Zyrus Press by:
Bryan Stoughton

About the Author

Mike Byers is president of Byers Numismatic Corp., a California corporation dealing in numismatics and the largest dealer of the world's rarest mint errors. He specializes in major U.S. and world mint errors, as well as die trials. A professional numismatist for over 30 years, Mr. Byers has handled many coin collections and attends every major coin convention. As a full time numismatist, Mr. Byers maintains a large inventory, solicits want lists and is always looking to purchase fresh inventory and collections.

In the last decade, Mr. Byers has made more discoveries of major mint errors both in the United States and around the world than any other dealer.

Included in Mr. Byers' premier inventory of mint errors and die trials are many discovery pieces which have been featured on the front page of *Coin World*, the world's #1 publication for coin collectors.

Coin World published the following coins that Mr. Byers discovered as front page articles:

- 1999 State Quarters Struck on experimental planchets certified by PCGS

- Transitional Sacagawea and Susan B Anthony Dollars certified by PCGS

- Martha Washington Cent Test Piece certified by NGC

- Canadian Cent struck with two reverse dies certified by PCGS

- 1910 Lincoln Cent Uniface Test Strike certified by PCGS

- Unique 1920 Buffalo Nickel struck in copper certified by NGC

Other discoveries by Mr. Byers that were also featured in *Coin World* include:

- State Quarters and other denominations struck on feeder finger tips certified by PCGS & NGC

- Additional Martha Washington Test Pieces in several different denominations certified by NGC

- The only known State Quarter Dual Date, Dual State certified by ANACS

- An assortment of world coins struck with either two obverse or two reverse dies certified by NGC & ANACS

Additional discoveries by Mr. Byers featured as cover stories in different issues of *Mint Error News Magazine* include:

- Unique 1866 $2½ struck on a 3 Cent Nickel planchet certified by NGC

- 1804 $2½ Capped Bust Double Struck certified by NGC

- 1806 $5 Capped Bust Triple Struck certified by PCGS

- Canadian Cent Die Cap with two reverse dies certified by PCGS

- 1971 ½ Pence Great Britain struck with two obverse dies Cu-Ni certified by NGC

- Unique Jefferson Nickel Die Trial by De Francisci certified by PCGS

- Unique Five Piece "Two Tailed" Euro Set certified by ANACS

- 1989-D Lincoln Cent Transitional Double Struck on bronze planchet certified by ICG

- Unique 3¢ Nickel struck on 1¢ Stock certified by NGC

In 1999, Mr. Byers launched *mikebyers.com*. Today it is the most widely viewed and informative mint error website on the Internet. The website has over 650 pages filled with articles, discoveries, breaking news and thousands of images of the most spectacular and dramatic major mint errors available in the market.

In 2003, Mr. Byers launched *minterrornews.com*, a website devoted to bringing the latest mint error news and information to the collector. Mr. Byers also serves as Editor of *minterrornews.com*. Today, *minterrornews.com* features articles, discoveries, news stories and mint error related information from the United States and around the world. *Minterrornews.com* became so popular that a print version, *Mint Error News Magazine*, was created by Mr. Byers and is read by thousands of readers. Mr. Byers also serves as the Publisher and Editor of *Mint Error News Magazine*. In addition to his extensive involvement in publishing on the subject of mint errors, Mr. Byers also served as a consultant to ANACS for mint errors from 2000 to 2006.

Mr. Byers is a life member of ANA since 1985, a charter member of NGC and a featured dealer/member of PCGS. He is a founder member of the California Coin & Precious Metals Association. He is also a life member of the Central States Numismatic Society, the Florida United Numismatists and a member of ICTA. He is member A71 in the Certified Coin Exchange (CCE).

When Mr. Byers isn't at coin conventions buying and selling mint errors he is usually in his office with customers or editing the next issue of his magazine or catalog.

His other interests and hobbies include snow skiing, playing the piano, traveling in Europe and racing sports cars.

Credits and Acknowledgements

I would like to express appreciation to the following individuals and companies for their assistance, contribution and participation with the creation of this book.

Fred Weinberg (fredweinberg.com)
Allan Levy (alscoins.com)
Heritage Auction Galleries (ha.com)
Saul Teichman (uspatterns.com)
Andy Lustig
C. Gutierrez
Phillip Taylor
Rick LaMont
Bart Crane
Uriah Cho
Ronnah Johnson
Sam Rhazi (mikebyers.com & minterrornews.com Web Design)
Mike Faraone
Dave Camire
Rich Schemmer
Jeff Ambio

Table of Contents

Preface

In 1975, I purchased a 1900 Indian Head Cent struck on a $2½ Indian gold blank planchet from the Beck Collection for $7,750 at a major coin auction. That price ranked among the top five ever realized by a mint error and represented a sum of money that few dealers or serious collectors would even consider spending on an error coin. Back then, there were no price guides for mint errors and very little information readily available to the public. Certainly there were no books to guide the reader through the vivid array and variety of mint error coinage.

Since then, the mint error market has witnessed an explosion in collector interest. Today, there are hundreds of dealers, investors and collectors who are purchasing major mint errors far in excess of $7,750. Much has changed since 1975, and in large part, the driving motivation behind this book was to assemble in one place the mint errors that best represent the culmination and maturity of mint error coinage as a fundamental segment of the overall numismatic market.

When I reflect back over the years, there are a number of important factors that come to mind that have contributed most to the emergence of mint errors in the numismatic market.

In 1991, the American Numismatic Association Certification Service (ANACS), one of the major coin grading and authenticating services, was the first to authenticate, grade and encapsulate major mint errors. They set a standard that not only established mint errors as a numismatic category, but also set a foundation upon which people could rely on when purchasing certified major mint errors. Then, in 1999, the Professional Coin Grading Service (PCGS) and the Numismatic Guaranty Corporation (NGC) started to certify mint errors as well, followed thereafter by The Independent Coin Grading Company (ICG). Major mint errors are now pursued, collected and traded just like patterns, territorial gold, colonials and other interesting segments of numismatics.

In addition to the impact of grading services on the mint error segment, the U.S. Mint instituted new programs that had the affect of attracting Americans to the collectibles market. The Mint's brilliantly implemented State Quarter program, in which five new designs of each state and territory were released for 11 years, along with the Presidential Dollar program, has introduced millions to coin collecting—and many of those collectors started out by searching for State Quarter mint errors.

In 2000, the U.S. Mint struck a record setting 28 billion coins across all denominations. This represents an incredible number of coins and contributed to the unintentional release, through normal distribution channels, of many new mint errors, including scores of State Quarter errors that gained the attention of national media outlets.

The discovery by collectors of these new State Quarter errors, along with mint errors from other denominations, added fuel to the mint error market. It seemed like many lucky collectors were finding an off-center State Quarter, an off-center Lincoln Cent, a State Quarter with copper on one side (missing clad layer) or a broadstruck Susan B. Anthony Dollar.

These and other major mint errors found their way into headline news of many publications including *Coin World, Numismatic News, Coinage Magazine, The Coin Dealer Newsletter* and *The Mint Error Newsletter.* The most spectacular and dramatic mint errors were reported through national media outlets. For example, in 2000, a small number of mules (coins produced by mismatched dies) were struck by the U.S. Mint. They featured a State Quarter obverse and Sacagawea Dollar reverse. This major discovery made national news and several of the 10 known specimens have subsequently sold for approximately $75,000 each. Today they are valued at approximately $100,000 each.

The prominence of mint errors in the public eye coincided in time with the rapidly expanding Internet. More and more people purchased computers and familiarized themselves with this new technology. Millions of collectors were instantaneously connected via the Web. The online auction website eBay® seemed to arise overnight as a major medium for coin transactions, and now rivals major auctions and coin shows. For the first time in history, dealers, investors and collectors could bid for major errors from behind a computer, something that would have been impossible not even 10 years ago without attending a live auction or coin show.

Experienced collectors with established coin collections also contributed to the growth of the mint error market. Collectors who grow weary of searching for coins by date, mintmark, denomination, or collecting in a pre-determined fashion by set or type often seek out new collecting prospects. This group contributed, and still contributes, to a core collector base that seeks out major mint errors. It is not uncommon for a serious collector of non-mint errors to add a major mint error with a value of $20,000 to $200,000 to an existing coin collection.

For collectors who choose to purchase rare and unique mint errors, a primary consideration is generally rarity and value. With mint errors, rarity is almost always extremely high. By way of example, take a U.S. 1879 Proof gold Stella with a mintage of 425 pieces. Clearly this is a rarity. Now, compare this coin to the double struck $20 Liberty mint error coin with a known quantity of ONE. Just one, which by definition makes it the quintessential definition of the word rare! The first coin sells for around $200,000 in Proof 65 condition, and the second recently sold for $102,500.

With that said, the window of opportunity to find new mint errors narrows each day. The first reason is obvious: a favorable change in market conditions has simply increased collector knowledge, interest and demand for mint errors. The second reason may be less obvious, and is an unintended consequence of the sheer quantity of coins struck by the Mint in the first part of the 21st century. The Federal Government has taken drastic measures to eliminate the flow of major mint errors in the normal run of production and distribution. Errors struck at the Mint are now locked in boxes until they are destroyed. Access to them is strictly limited. Additional riddlers have been installed and have caught many of the errors that previously passed through. Counting rooms have been warned that their contracts would not be renewed unless every mint error that is discovered is returned.

The net effect of the growing demand and dwindling supply suggests that the price increases seen in the market could continue. As I write this, several dealers need thousands of off-center nickels and dimes, and are willing to pay top-dollar for such coins. On the other end of the spectrum, error dealers like me pay thousands of dollars for rare type errors and spectacular unique errors.

This is an exciting time for mint errors, and an even more exciting time to be a mint error collector. The combination of the major grading services certifying error coins, the rise of the Internet as a medium for collectors to buy and sell, the dramatic impact of new U.S. Mint programs, along with record setting mintage figures have all contributed to an explosion of interest in mint errors and their acceptance as a vital component of the modern numismatic market.

I look forward to what the future will bring to the world of mint error collecting. And, as the mint error market continues to grow, expand and change, it is my hope that this guide will be one that collectors will refer back to time and time again as a valuable and important contribution to the mint error segment of numismatics.

Introduction

World's Greatest Mint Errors is the first book ever published to focus specifically on the most spectacular error coins from the United States Mint and mints throughout the world. While the primary attraction of this book will be found in the hundreds of large scale, full color error coin images, some which have never before been published, its practical application for the numismatist will be as a guide toward a better understanding of major mint errors, their relative rarity, and value.

Many coins found within these pages are so unique that they have eluded widespread exposure in numismatic circles. With the "best of the best" in mint errors presented in one visually attractive and informative format, it is likely that the specialized collector will discover a number of significant pieces that would serve well as a centerpiece for their collection. Likewise, generalized collectors will gain a deeper insight into these truly rare coins and, through that understanding, an appreciation for this exciting segment of the numismatic market.

To help place error coins in the proper context in the numismatic market of the early 21st century, you will also find within this book up-to-date rarity estimates and values for each coin featured. These rarity estimates are based predominantly on my own experiences buying, selling and studying error coins over the course of 30 plus years as a professional numismatist. For each specimen, the rarity estimates are given for that specific kind of error for coins of that specific type. Take for example a rarity estimate of 10 coins known for a broadstruck 1929-S Standing Liberty Quarter. This estimate means that there are only 10 broadstruck Standing Liberty Quarters of the Type II design (1917-1930) known. Remember that many of the errors pictured in this book are unique in relation to the specific issue on which they were struck. Additionally, all errors are unique when we consider that no two pieces look exactly alike.

In addition to values for each individual piece pictured in this book, you will also find more general price guides for many types of errors on both modern mint coinage and pieces from the 20th and earlier centuries. These general price guides, found at the end of most chapters, were compiled with the help of leading error coin dealers. These dealers handle errors and experimental pieces on a daily basis, and their expertise in determining the rarity and value is unsurpassed in the market.

Even so, the price guides in this book are just that: guides. Prices for major mint errors and experimental pieces vary according to the type of coin, issue, grade, eye appeal and other factors. They also fluctuate with general market and economic conditions such as supply and demand and the general state of the economy. Prices can vary dramatically simply because two collectors eager to own the same coin bid the price up at auction.

Any purchase, especially a purchase of a major mint error, should be preceded by research and study. I recommend using multiple printed resources, prices realized, records from recent auctions, and to seek the advice of as many recognized experts in the dealer community as possible. These experts often have knowledge of changing and evolving market conditions that are not yet represented in books, magazines, auction records and other printed and archival sources.

Mint error coins are an exciting segment of the numismatic market. Simply put, no other coins are more intriguing, fascinating, or visually dramatic. My enthusiasm for major mint errors has continued unabated for over 30 years, and it is my hope that you too will grow to share my excitement for these coins as you read and study this book. May the information presented in the following pages prove useful, educational and enjoyable as you expand your understanding of and appreciation for these most unusual coins.

Chapter 1

Bonded Coins

Bonded coin errors are created when the feeder system that supplies blank planchets to the press jams or otherwise malfunctions. When this occurs, a struck coin is not ejected, another planchet is fed into the press on top of it and both are struck together. The malfunction of the feeder system can affect multiple planchets, creating some truly exceptional bonded coin errors with three, four or even more planchets.

1.

1964 Kennedy Half Dollar
Two-Piece Bonded Die Cap—MS-65

This amazing two-piece bonded die cap is the only such error known from the 90% silver Kennedy Half Dollar series of 1964. The obverse die cap is 1/3 off-center, and it is bonded to another planchet that was struck multiple times while serving as a reverse die cap. This dramatic mint error is larger than a Silver Dollar.

Rarity: Unique
Value: $20,000

2.

1999-P Bonded Connecticut Statehood Quarters
Two-Piece Die Cap—MS-65

This important error is one of only four bonded pairs known from the entire Statehood Quarter series. The error occurred when two planchets were fed into the collar at the same time. Neither planchet was properly centered when the dies came together, thus creating an impressive, large-size error.

Bonded pairs are occasionally discovered in the Cent denomination, and much less so in the Nickel and Dime denominations. On the other hand, such errors are extremely rare in larger denominations such as Quarters and Half Dollars. The present example is of even further importance due to the popularity of the Statehood Quarter series as a whole. This series has become so popular, in fact, that many error collectors are trying to assemble sets of one error from each of the 50 state issues.

Rarity: 4 Known
Value: $7,500

3.

1999-P Pennsylvania Statehood Quarter

Two-Piece Bonded Die Cap—MS-65

Even more dramatic than the bonded 1999-P Connecticut Statehood Quarter pair listed on the facing page, this Pennsylvania example is actually one of the most desirable mint errors of any type discovered in recent years. Similar to the 1964 Kennedy Half Dollar, the error on this 1999-P Pennsylvania Quarter is a combination of a multi-struck obverse die cap and a bonded pair.

Rarity: 3 Known
Value: $7,500

4.

Sweden, 1964 2 Ore, KM-821

Bonded to a Wrench—As Struck

A unique and spectacular error, this piece was apparently created when a Mint employee used a wrench in an attempt to clear a jam in the coinage press. Unfortunately (or fortunately, depending on your point of view), the employee did not stop the press before inserting the wrench. The tool was caught between the dies when they came together and struck into a planchet.

Although I am aware of a few world coins bonded to washers, nails and other small tool parts, this 1964 Swedish 2 Ore is the only error known that includes a wrench.

Rarity: Unique
Value: $7,500

5.

1999-P Roosevelt Dime

Three-Piece Bonded Die Cap—ANACS MS-65

This Roosevelt Dime is an obverse die cap that consists of three bonded planchets. Obviously struck many times while capping the die, the planchets expanded so much that they have split in several areas. The resulting error is the size of a Silver Dollar – an impressive characteristic for planchets that started out the size of a Dime!

Although rare, two-piece bonded planchets are encountered now and then in the error coin segment of the numismatic market. The same cannot, however, be said for bonded errors that include more than two planchets. Indeed, this important Roosevelt Dime is one of no more than 10 errors of the type believed to exist.

Rarity: 10 Known
Value: $3,000

14

6.

Undated Roosevelt Dime
Multi-Struck Bonded Pair—NGC MS-65

Struck multiple times on two bonded planchets, this is an exciting error from the Roosevelt Dime series. Finding bonded coins in denominations above Cents are rare.

Rarity: 10-20 Known
Value: $2,000

Price Guide for Bonded Coins

Denomination	2 Planchets	3-4 Planchets
Lincoln Cent Wheat Ears	$5,000	$15,000
Lincoln Cent Memorial	$1,500	$3,500
Jefferson Nickel	$2,000	$5,000
Roosevelt Dime Silver	$4,000	$12,500
Roosevelt Dime Clad	$2,500	$5,000
Washington Quarter Silver	$7,500	–
Washington Quarter Clad	$2,000	–
State Quarter	$5,000	–
Kennedy Half Silver	$20,000	–
Kennedy Half Clad	$10,000	–
Eisenhower Dollar	–	–
Susan B Anthony Dollar	–	–
Sacagawea Dollar	–	–

Chapter 2

Broadstrikes

A broadstruck error occurs when a coin is struck in the absence of the collar. The collar forms the rim and edge of a coin and ensures that it emerges from the press with the proper shape and diameter. When the collar is absent or in an incorrect position, the coin will become distorted and expand dramatically since there is nothing to contain the extreme pressure generated by the press during striking.

Coins can be broadstruck on either Type I or Type II planchets. Many broadstruck coins are also examples of other types of mint errors. For example, many broadstruck coins are also double or triple struck, or have indents from other planchets.

1.

1906-D Liberty Double Eagle
Broadstruck—NGC AU-58

Although the visual characteristics of this error are difficult to see because the coin is mounted in an NGC holder, this Double Eagle is broadstruck out of the collar. There is no reeding on the edge, and the planchet has expanded so that the coin is larger than the size of a properly struck Liberty Double Eagle.

The Mint usually devoted considerable time and effort to inspecting large-denomination coins for errors, and this is particularly true for gold coins. Very few Double Eagle errors of any kind escaped the careful scrutiny of Mint employees—a fact that confirms the rarity of this important piece.

Rarity: Unique
Value: $40,000

2.

1852-D Liberty Half Eagle
Broadstruck—NGC AU-58

At first glance, this coin has the appearance of an off-center error. All peripheral design elements are present, however, so the error is properly classified as an uncentered broadstrike. That is, the planchet was not properly centered in the press when it was struck. The collar was absent at the time of striking, hence the coin's greater-than-normal diameter. A challenging error to find on a Liberty Half Eagle regardless of date and issuing mint, the fact that this coin is a product of the Dahlonega Mint means that it has tremendous appeal for a wide variety of collectors including Southern gold specialists and error collectors.

Rarity: Unique
Value: $30,000

3.

1893-O Liberty Eagle
Broadstruck—PCGS AU-58

Another impressive example of a broadstruck error on a Liberty gold coin, this 1893-O Eagle was not seated in the collar when the dies came together during striking. The reeding around the edge is missing, and the diameter is greater than that which is normal for properly struck Liberty Eagles.

In addition to its status as a gold coin error, this 1893-O Eagle is of profound significance to specialized collectors because very few error coins of any kind are known from the New Orleans Mint.

Rarity: Unique
Value: $25,000

4.

1999 Susan B. Anthony Dollar
Broadstruck, Multi-Struck Die Cap—PCGS MS-65

This Anthony Dollar appears to have been struck at least four times. The first impression occurred in the absence of the collar – a broadstrike error. The coin was then struck a second time, at which point it became a reverse die cap. The obverse was then struck into another blank planchet at least once, at which time the detail on Anthony's portrait became flat and distended. The planchet eventually freed itself from the reverse die, but was struck one final time before leaving the press. This "exit" strike is present on both sides of the planchet, and it is 80% off-center.

The multiple strikes that created this error have caused the coin to expand to the size of a Morgan Silver Dollar. This is the largest Anthony Dollar error of any kind that I have ever seen, and it is amazing that this piece escaped the attention of Mint employees tasked with discovering such errors before they are released into general circulation.

> *Rarity: 5 Known*
> *Value: $7,500*

5.

1886 Gold Dollar
Broadstruck—NGC MS-64

This Type III Gold Dollar is an uncentered broadstrike. Most broadstruck U.S. gold coin errors are circulated, even if only lightly. This Gem 1886 Gold Dollar, however, has been carefully preserved since the day of striking. Apparently, someone living in the United States during 1886 (perhaps an employee in the Philadelphia Mint or a bank teller) recognized the error and set this coin aside before it acquired any wear from circulation. This rarely happened with gold errors from the 19th and early 20th centuries because the coins had such tremendous buying power during the years in which they were in production at the Mint.

> *Rarity: 5 Known*
> *Value: $5,000*

6.

1934 Walking Liberty Half Dollar

Broadstruck—ANACS MS-60

All Walking Liberty Half Dollar errors are extremely rare coins. This broadstruck 1934 is of even greater significance because the error has resulted in a considerably larger diameter for the coin. Additionally, the 1934 is a more challenging issue to locate than the common-date issues from the World War II era such as the 1941, 1942 or 1943.

Rarity: 5 Known
Value: $5,000

7.

1929-S Standing Liberty Quarter

Broadstruck—PCGS MS-62

This broadstruck 1929-S Standing Liberty Quarter has expanded greatly in size and displays an overlay of light, original toning that further enhances the eye appeal. The Standing Liberty Quarter is a very rare type to find as a major mint error.

Rarity: 10 Known
Value: $4,500

8.

Undated Jefferson Nickel
Broadstruck, Obverse Off-Center Double Brockage—ANACS MS-63

There are two off-center brockages on the obverse of this Jefferson Nickel. The multiple impressions that this coin received occurred outside of the collar, with the result that the error has expanded to the size of a Half Dollar. The stress on the planchet has also resulted in a dramatic split at 7-8 o'clock at the obverse rim.

The Jefferson Nickel series is one of the most prolific for major mint errors. Even so, very few Jefferson Nickel errors that have escaped the Mint are as dramatic as this off-center brockage.

Rarity: 100+ Known
Value: $250

Price Guide for Broadstrikes

Denomination	(Small) XF/AU	(Small) Unc	(Large) XF/AU	(Large) Unc
Large Cent	$150	$300	$400	$1,500
Flying Eagle Cent (1857–1858)	$1,000	$2,500	$1,500	$7,500
Indian Cent	$50	$150	$200	$350
Lincoln Cent 1930 and Earlier	$50	$150	$100	$250
Lincoln Cent 1943 Steel	$40	$100	$75	$200
Proof Lincoln Cent	N/A	$1,500	N/A	$2,500
3 Cent Nickel	$250	$1,000	$400	$1,500
3 Cent Silver	$1,000	$3,500	$1,500	$5,000
Shield Nickel	$400	$1,250	$1,000	$2,500
Liberty Nickel	$150	$300	$200	$600
Buffalo Nickel	$100	$200	$200	$500
Jefferson Nickel War Time	$100	$200	$200	$500
Proof Jefferson Nickel	N/A	$2,500	N/A	$4,000
Seated Half Dime Legend	$1,500	$3,500	$2,000	$7,500
Seated Dime Legend	$1,500	$3,500	$2,000	$7,500
Barber Dime	$150	$250	$200	$400
Mercury Dime	$40	$150	$150	$250
Proof Clad Dime	N/A	$3,000	N/A	$5,000
Barber Quarter	$600	$1,250	$1,000	$2,500
Standing Liberty Quarter	$2,000	$4,000	$3,000	$6,000
Washington Quarter Silver	$75	$150	$100	$250
State Quarter	N/A	$25	N/A	$50
Proof Clad Quarter	N/A	$4,000	N/A	$5,000
Barber Half	$2,500	$3,500	$3,000	$5,000
Walking Liberty Half	$3,000	$5,000	$4,000	$7,000
Franklin Half	$1,500	$3,000	$2,000	$4,000
Kennedy Half Silver	$150	$250	$200	$300
Kennedy Half Clad	$40	$60	$50	$75
Proof Clad Half	N/A	$5,000	N/A	$7,000
Morgan Dollar	$200	$500	$400	$1,000
Peace Dollar	$4,000	$6,000	$6,000	$10,000
Eisenhower Dollar	$100	$150	$150	$200
Susan B Anthony Dollar	$50	$75	$100	$200
Sacagawea Dollar	N/A	$300	N/A	$500
Presidential Dollar	N/A	$1,500	N/A	$2,500

Chapter 3

Brockages

B *rockage errors can only be created when there are two planchets involved. One of the planchets will always be a struck coin that has not properly ejected from the press. This struck coin will find its way back between the dies and either the obverse or the reverse will be struck into a blank planchet that is subsequently fed into the collar. The image of the struck coin will be impressed into the blank planchet, the result of which will be a second struck coin with the proper image on one side and an incuse, inverted image of the previously struck coin on the other. This incuse, inverted image is a brockage.*

1874 Gold Dollar

Obverse Full-Mirror Brockage—PCGS MS-62

This incredible and unique Type III Gold Dollar is a first-strike mirror brockage, and it is one of the most spectacular mint errors of any kind. The error was created when a struck coin remained in the press, either loose or as an obverse die cap. A second planchet was then fed into the press and, while the reverse received a proper impression from that die, the obverse was struck with the reverse of the previously struck coin. The obverse of this error, therefore, depicts an incuse, mirror-image impression of the reverse design of the Type III Gold Dollar.

This dramatic piece is the only known full brockage on a Type III Gold Dollar. It is also one of only two brockages discovered on a United States gold coin of any denomination or type. The coin is fully Mint State with lovely prooflike surfaces.

Rarity: Unique
Value: $150,000

2.

1806 and 1806/5 Draped Bust Quarters

Obverse (B-2, Rarity-4 as a Die Variety) and
Reverse (B-1, Rarity-2 as a Die Variety)
Full-Mirror Brockage Pair—PCGS VF-30

These mirror brockages on a pair of 1806 Draped Bust Quarters are the earliest known errors of this type on any silver denomination struck in the United States Mint. The obverse brockage is attributed to the reverse die of the 1806 Browning-2 variety. The reverse brockage, however, is matched to the obverse die of the 1806/5 Browning-1 variety.

Rare and challenging types to collect even when properly struck, the Draped and Capped Bust Quarter series have yielded very few major mint errors of any kind. This 1806 and 1806/5 Draped Bust pair is unique for a brockage error in the entire Bust Quarter series of 1796-1838.

Rarity: Unique
Value: $100,000

3.

Undated San Francisco Mint Barber Half Dollar

Obverse Full-Mirror Brockage—PCGS AU-58

This full mirror brockage is unique for an error of this type in the Barber Half Dollar series. Since it is an obverse brockage, the year in which this coin was struck is unknown. The S mintmark is readily evident, however, so this error is definitely a product of the San Francisco Mint.

Nearly Mint State, this piece retains virtually full mint luster that includes appreciable reflectivity in the fields. Both sides are extremely smooth with an overlay of original golden-brown toning.

Rarity: Unique
Value: $50,000

4.

Undated Large Size Capped Bust Dime

Obverse Full-Mirror Brockage—NGC MS-64

This Capped Bust Dime error exhibits a full mirror brockage on the obverse. Major Mint errors of any kind are seldom seen on Large Size Capped Bust Dimes of 1809-1828. This important example is also a carefully preserved near-Gem with solid technical quality and strong eye appeal.

Rarity: Unique
Value: $40,000

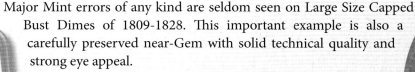

5.

1843-C Liberty Quarter Eagle

Partial Brockage—PCGS AU-58

A fascinating coin, this error was created when a struck coin did not fully eject from the press. When another planchet was inserted between the dies, the previously struck coin came to rest over part of the blank after it was seated in the collar. The subsequent strike from the dies imparted most of the proper design to the planchet in the collar, but it also resulted in the formation of a small (5%) partial brockage from the previously struck coin at 12 o'clock on the obverse.

This major mint error is rare not only because it is a gold coin, but also because it is a product of the Charlotte Mint. The coin is virtually Mint State with bright, nearly fully intact luster.

Rarity: Unique
Value: $25,000

6.

1829 Large Cent
Reverse Full-Mirror Brockage—PCGS AU-55

A first-strike, full-mirror brockage, this early-date Coronet Cent displays two dates! Most brockages in the large Cent series are obverse brockages, and the coins tend to be heavily circulated with impairments such as scratched and corrosion. The 1829 pictured here is not only a rare reverse brockage, but it is problem-free with only light wear to the highpoints. This example clearly has tremendous appeal not only among error specialists, but also for early Copper collectors.

Rarity: 10 Known
Value: $12,500

7.

Undated Two-Cent Piece
Obverse Full Brockage—PCGS MS-63 Red and Brown

This Two-Cent brockage appears to be an approximately third or fourth strike from a capped die. The incuse reverse design that is present on the obverse of this error is flat and distended. In fact, only the wreath and the denomination 2 CENTS are visible. Had this coin been a full mirror brockage, the entire incuse reverse design would be visible. The obverse die cap had obviously struck a few other planchets before it became involved in the creation of this particular example.

The Two-Cent series of 1864-1873 has yielded very few major mint errors. This "almost-mirror" brockage is fully Uncirculated with considerable portion of mint-red luster remaining.

Rarity: 5 Known
Value: $10,000

8.

Undated Three-Cent Silver
Obverse Full-Mirror Brockage—PCGS AU-58

A full-mirror brockage is seen on the obverse of this fascinating Three-Cent Silver. The date is missing, of course, but the inclusion of the olive sprig and bundle of arrows as part of the reverse design confirm this error as either a Type II or Type III Trime from 1854-1873.

The brevity of the Three-Cent Silver series and the fact that the denomination was in production at a time when there was little, if any numismatic interest in error coins explain the rarity of such pieces in today's market. This obverse full-mirror brockage is nearly Mint State with virtually full luster.

> *Rarity: 5 Known*
> *Value: $7,500*

9.

Rome, Augustus (BC 27-AD 14), Undated (BC 19-18) AR Denarius, Pergamum, Sear-1591, RIC-516, BMCRE-672, RSC-11
Reverse Full-Mirror Brockage—ICG EF-40

A rare type even when properly struck, this Roman Denarius of Caesar Augustus is unique as a reverse full-mirror brockage error.

Although there are many brockage errors known on ancient silver coins, the majority are examples of the more common types.

> *Rarity: Unique*
> *Value: $5,000*

10.

Byzantine, Justin II (AD 565-578), Undated (AD 565-578) AV Tremissis, Sear-353

Reverse Full-Mirror Brockage—ICG AU-58

An incuse impression from the obverse die is present on the reverse of this Byzantine AV Tremissis from the reign of Justin II. The sharp detail to the brockage indicates that it is a first strike.

There are only two first-strike full mirror brockage errors known on ancient gold coins. This Byzantine example is nearly in the Mint State category, and it is a coin that would serve as a highlight of any specialized collection.

Rarity: Unique
Value: $5,000

11.

Undated Kennedy Half Dollar

Obverse Indent and Partial Brockage—NGC MS-64

Combining multiple errors in the coining process, this Kennedy Half Dollar is one of the most visually impressive errors of the type. A smaller planchet (Nickel or Dime?) was accidentally fed into the Half Dollar press and struck by the dies. The planchet failed to eject from the press and, when the next planchet was inserted between the dies, the previously struck coin was impressed into the Half Dollar.

Rarity: 5 Known
Value: $5,000

12.

Great Britain, 1853 ½ Sovereign, Spink-3859

Reverse Full-Mirror Brockage—ANACS MS-60

A first-strike reverse full mirror brockage confirms this coin as a rare and exciting British gold error from the reign of Queen Victoria. This piece is the earliest-dated brockage error known on a ½ Sovereign.

Rarity: Unique
Value: $5,000

13.

Undated Indian Cent

Reverse Off-Center Mirror Brockage—NGC MS-62 Brown

Struck 35% off-center at 5 o'clock, this undated Indian Cent also displays a first-strike brockage on the reverse. It is unusual for a coin of any denomination or type to combine these two errors, but modern U.S. coins such as Lincoln Cents and Jefferson Nickels are encountered once in a while in numismatic circles. Early types such as the Indian Cent are extremely rare with this double error.

Rarity: 5 Known
Value: $3,500

14.

Byzantine, Phocas (AD 602-610), Undated (AD 602-610) AV Solidus, Sear-620

Overstruck on Full Reverse Brockage—ICG MS-63

This Phocas Gold Solidus was struck over a full reverse brockage. Remnants of the brockage are still noticeable underneath the overstrike. The second strike is slightly off-center. Both sides possess exceptionally sharp definition to the devices.

Rarity: 5 Known
Value: $3,500

15.

Netherlands, Undated 10 Gulden, Fr-347

Reverse Full-Mirror Brockage—ANACS AU-58

The obverse design that this 10 Gulden piece exhibits was used to strike coins dated 1892, 1895 and 1897. Given the extreme rarity of the 1892 and 1895, this error probably occurred on an 1897. Minimally worn, this coin possesses bold detail and problem-free surfaces. Gold brockages are very rare.

Rarity: Unique
Value: $3,000

16.

Undated Indian Cent
Struck Through Capped Die—PCGS MS-64 Brown

This interesting error is struck three times from an obverse die cap, the multiple impressions resulting in a flat, distended appearance to the incuse brockage on the obverse. There is also evidence of the various different strikes on the reverse around the outlines of the shield, wreath and the letters in the denomination ONE CENT. Apparently, the coin rotated ever so slightly in the collar between impressions.

Certified by PCGS, this attractive near-Gem possesses rich copper-brown patina and modest semi-prooflike qualities to the surfaces.

Rarity: 20 Known
Value: $3,000

17.

Great Britain, Undated ½ Sovereign, Spink-3860
Obverse Full-Mirror Brockage—ANACS MS-63

The reverse design with the die number at the lower rim confirms the basic Spink-3860 attribution, and it also dates this error to the 18-year period from 1863 through 1880. Another first-strike brockage, the obverse of this coin displays an incuse impression of the reverse design. Although struck on a later type than the 1853 example, this error is still highly desirable due to the infrequency with which major mint errors are encountered on British ½ Sovereigns of any type.

Rarity: Unique
Value: $2,500

18.

Isle of Man, Undated 1/20 Noble, KM-266
Obverse Full-Mirror Brockage—ANACS Proof-64

Major errors on platinum coins from any country are all but unknown, examples struck in this metal almost always being made with extreme care on the part of the issuing Mint. This spectacular and unique 1/20 Noble from the Isle of Man was prepared in proof format. Although such coins are usually subject to careful scrutiny before leaving the Mint, this piece escaped as a first-strike brockage error with the entire reverse design incuse on the obverse.

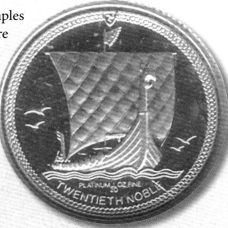

Rarity: Unique
Value: $2,500

19.

Undated Philadelphia Mint Statehood Quarter
Obverse Die Cap Reverse Brockage—ANACS MS-66

The planchet capped the obverse die and probably imparted an obverse brockage of the reverse design into one or more additional blank planchets that were subsequently fed into the press. These multiple impressions eventually obliterated the reverse design of the die cap, at which point a previously struck Statehood Quarter found its way back into the collar with the obverse up. The die cap was then struck into that coin creating an incuse brockage of the obverse design. Any coins subsequently struck from this die cap would be counterbrockages (see Chapter 4 for more information on errors of that type).

This State Quarter Die Cap is super deep and has a brockage reverse. It barely fits in the ANACS slab and is very dramatic.

Rarity: 20 Known
Value: $1,500

20.

Undated Susan B. Anthony Dollar
Obverse Off-Center Partial Brockage—ANACS MS-64

Struck approximately 80% off-center at 11 o'clock, this coin also displays a partial brockage on the obverse. The error has resulted in a flat, distended area on the planchet where you can see both the obverse brockage and a small portion of the reverse design. The balance of the planchet is blank, thereby giving the error an even more dramatic appearance.

The Anthony Dollar series of 1979-1999 has resulted in the creation of many off-center errors. Only a small number of those coins, however, are also brockages.

Rarity: 10 Known
Value: $1,500

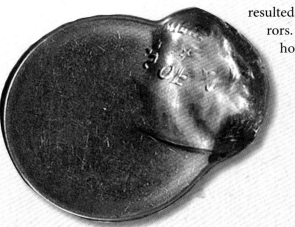

Price Guide for Brockages

Denomination	50% Brockage XF	100% Brockage XF	50% Brockage Unc	100% Brockage Unc
Large Cent	$600	$1,000	$3,000	$10,000
Indian Cent	$500	$1,250	$1,500	$4,000
Lincoln Cent 1943 Steel	$350	$500	$650	$1,000
Lincoln Cent Wheat Ears	$125	$200	$200	$350
3 Cent Nickel	$1,250	$2,000	$3,500	$5,000
3 Cent Silver	$2,000	$3,000	$3,000	$6,000
Shield Nickel	$1,500	$2,500	$3,500	$5,000
Liberty Nickel	$1,250	$2,250	$2,000	$4,000
Buffalo Nickel	$2,000	$2,500	$2,500	$7,500
Jefferson Nickel War Time	$250	$750	$750	$1,500
Jefferson Nickel	$50	$75	$50	$150
Barber Dime	$2,500	$3,500	$5,000	$12,500
Mercury Dime	$1,000	$3,000	$1,500	$4,000
Roosevelt Dime Silver	$100	$200	$150	$250
Roosevelt Dime Clad	$50	$100	$75	$150
Washington Quarter Silver	$200	$500	$500	$1,000
Washington Quarter Clad	$75	$150	$150	$250
State Quarter	N/A	N/A	$750	$1,500
Kennedy Half Clad	N/A	N/A	$650	$1,500
Eisenhower Dollar	$1,500	$2,500	$3,000	$7,500
Susan B Anthony Dollar	N/A	N/A	$500	$1,500
Sacagawea Dollar	N/A	N/A	$1,500	$4,000

Chapter 4

Counterbrockages

*C*ounterbrockage errors involve a die cap and a previously struck coin. When a die cap strikes a previously struck coin, the obverse design from that struck coin will be impressed into the cap, creating an incuse, inverted image (a brockage). When a new planchet is struck by the brockage on the die cap, that side of the planchet (usually the obverse) will acquire a raised, distended image from the brockage. The impression from the brockage is known as a counterbrockage.

The size and detail in the counterbrockage image vary depending on how many planchets are struck by the brockage on the die cap. Each subsequent impression creates a counter-brockage with larger devices and poorer definition than the preceding counter-brockage. Counterbrockages are often combined with other types of errors on the same coin, die cap or mated pair.

1.

1979 Kennedy Half Dollar—Mated Pair

Die Cap, Brockage and Counterbrockage Errors—ANACS MS-63

Unique as a mated pair, this set is representative of several major mint errors. The first example is a double-struck obverse die cap with a reverse double counterbrockage. The second piece is triple struck with an obverse double brockage.

Each of these Kennedy Half Dollars would represent a significant find were they discovered individually. The fact that they have been preserved together speaks volumes about their importance to error coin specialists.

Rarity: 2 Known
Value: $7,500

2.

Undated Liberty Nickel
Counterbrockage—ANACS MS-64

This coin is the only known counterbrockage error on a Liberty Nickel. The obverse displays a flat, distended design with Liberty's portrait essentially filling the entire area on that side. The reverse, on the other hand, received a normal strike from the die. A spectacular and unique major mint error, this piece is pictured on page 234 of the 2004 book *The Error Coin Encyclopedia*, Fourth Edition by Arnold Margolis and Fred Weinberg. It is also pictured in the 1966 book *The U.S. Mint and Coinage* by Don Taxay.

Rarity: Unique
Value: $5,000

Price Guide for Counterbrockages

Denomination	Circulated	AU	Unc	Choice Unc - Gem
Indian Cent	$1,000	$1,500	$2,000	$2,500
Lincoln Cent 1943 Steel	$500	$750	$1,500	$2,000
Lincoln Cent Wheat Ears	$200	$200	$300	$500
Lincoln Cent Memorial	$40	$50	$75	$100
Shield Nickel	$1,500	$2,000	$4,000	$5,000
Liberty Nickel	$1,500	$2,000	$4,000	$5,000
Jefferson Nickel	$50	$100	$150	$200
Barber Dime	$3,000	$5,000	$7,500	$10,000
Roosevelt Dime Silver	$300	$500	$750	$1,000
Roosevelt Dime Clad	$100	$150	$250	$300
Washington Quarter Silver	$500	$1,000	$1,500	$2,000
Washington Quarter Clad	$100	$200	$300	$400
State Quarter	N/A	$750	$1,250	$1,500
Kennedy Half Silver	$1,250	$2,000	$3,000	$4,000
Kennedy Half Clad	$500	$750	$1,250	$1,500
Susan B Anthony Dollar	N/A	$1,500	$2,000	$2,500

Chapter 5

Die Adjustment Strikes

D ie adjustment strikes are also known as die trials. This error occurs when a coin is struck from the press with very little pressure. When the press is being set up and adjusted, extremely weak strikes occur as the strike pressure reaches its optimum level. These die trials are destroyed after being struck and are rarely found in circulation.

Undated Peace Dollar
Die Adjustment Strike, Struck 25% Off-Center—PCGS AU-50

Not only is this coin a die adjustment strike error, but it is also struck 25% off-center at approximately 12 o'clock. This coin is the farthest off-center error known from the entire 1921-1935 Peace Dollar series. Additionally, it is one of only two die adjustment strike Peace Dollars that is also struck off center. Well known in numismatic circles for decades, this piece is a famous rarity that continues to enjoy strong demand among specialized collectors.

> *Rarity: 2 Known*
> *Value: $75,000*

2.

1923 Peace Dollar

Die Adjustment Strike, Struck 5% Off-Center—NGC-Certified

In addition to displaying die trial/weak strike and off-center errors, this 1923 Peace Dollar is broadstruck out of the collar. Only two of the die adjustment strike Peace Dollar errors that have been discovered are also struck off-center: the present example and the undated piece pictured below.

Rarity: 2 Known
Value: $10,000

3.

1922-S Peace Dollar

Die Adjustment Strike—PCGS MS-61

There was so little pressure in the press when this coin was struck that the lettering and detail at the rims is the only element of the design that is readily discernible. Closer inspection does reveal the faintest outline to Liberty's portrait in the center of the obverse. Free of wear, and accurately described as Mint State by PCGS.

Rarity: 5 Known
Value: $10,000

4.

1877 Seated Quarter
Die Adjustment Strike—NGC-Certified

This 1877 Quarter is the only die adjustment strike error known for any of the denominations (Half Dime through Silver Dollar) in the Seated Liberty coinage family. Significantly, and despite the overall lack of detail, the coin does include a relatively bold date. Portions of Liberty's portrait and the reverse eagle are also discernible.

Rarity: Unique
Value: $7,500

5.

Undated Walking Liberty Half Dollar
Die Adjustment Strike—PCGS AU-55

The only error of this type reported from the entire Walking Liberty Half Dollar series of 1916-1945, this piece was formerly part of the collection of a well-known East Coast coin dealer.

Rarity: Unique
Value: $5,000

Price Guide for Die Adjustment Strikes

Denomination	XF/AU	Unc
Indian Cent	$1,000	$2,000
Lincoln Cent Wheat Ear	$200	$300
Lincoln Cent 1943 Steel	$750	$1,500
Lincoln Cent Memorial	$50	$75
2 Cent	$5,000	–
Liberty Nickel	$3,000	$5,000
Buffalo Nickel	$4,000	$7,500
Jefferson Nickel War Time	$1,250	$2,000
Jefferson Nickel	$75	$100
Proof Jefferson Nickel	N/A	$4,000
Barber Dime	$2,500	$3,500
Mercury Dime	$1,000	$1,500
Roosevelt Dime Silver	$350	$500
Roosevelt Dime Clad	$100	$125
Seated Quarter	$5,000	$7,500
Standing Liberty Quarter	$15,000	$20,000
Washington Quarter Silver	$500	$750
Washington Quarter Clad (Pre-State)	$125	$150
State Quarter	N/A	$200
Walking Liberty Half	$2,500	$5,000
Kennedy Half Silver	$500	$750
Kennedy Half Clad	$200	$250
Proof Kennedy Half 40% Silver	N/A	$5,000
Proof Kennedy Half Clad	N/A	$4,000
Morgan Dollar	$5,000	$7,500
Peace Dollar	$10,000	$15,000
Eisenhower Dollar	$300	$400
Eisenhower Dollar Bicentennial	$350	$500
Susan B Anthony Dollar	N/A	$500
Sacagawea Dollar	N/A	$1,000

Chapter 6

Die Caps

*D*ie caps are caused when a struck coin adheres to the upper, or hammer die in the press. Once one side of the coin (usually the obverse) caps the die face, the other side (usually the reverse) becomes the new face of the die. When the next planchet is fed into the collar and is struck, the design of the die cap impresses itself into the planchet and creates a brockage. This process repeats itself as more planchets are struck by the cap. Each subsequent strike causes the metal around the edge of the die cap to be pushed further around the shaft of the die.

Eventually, the cap frees itself from the die, usually after assuming the shape of a bottle cap or thimble due to multiple impressions as a cap.

1.

1864 Two-Cent Piece

Mated Pair of an Obverse Die Cap and Obverse Brockage—
PCGS MS-62 Brown

It is amazing that this mated pair of Two-Cent piece errors survived intact since the penultimate year of the Civil War. The first example is an obverse die cap, while the second piece is an obverse brockage struck from that die cap. The die cap is so deep that it could not be sonically sealed in a PCGS holder. It is, however, accompanied by an official PCGS insert and photo proof confirming authenticity.

Major mint errors are seldom encountered in the Two-Cent series of 1864-1873. Of further importance for judging the rarity of this mated pair is that fact that there are only three pre-1940 die cap pairs known for all U.S. coin denominations.

Rarity: Unique
Value: $100,000

2.

New Orleans Mint Barber Dimes
Obverse and Reverse Die Caps—PCGS AU-55

Both of these die caps were struck in the New Orleans Mint, a coinage facility that has yielded very few error coins of any kind over the years. The obverse die cap is dated 1893, and it one of only five such errors attributed to the Barber Dime series. The reverse die cap is even rarer; in fact, it is unique for a coin of this type.

The bottle-cap shape that the obverse die cap has assumed includes particularly steep sides, and the coin barely fits within the PCGS holder in which it is mounted. The reverse of this piece is extremely distorted, obviously from producing numerous incuse brockages on other planchets that were fed into the press while the obverse die was capped.

Rarity: Unique (as a Pair)
Value: $75,000

3.

1856 Large Cent
Obverse Die Cap, Reverse Brockage—PCGS MS-64 Brown

The die cap is so deep that this coin could not fit in any of the holders currently being used by PCGS, NGC, ANACS or ICG. Such is the stress that the die cap created that the planchet has also split at 4 o'clock on the obverse rim. In addition to this planchet split, the reverse also displays a flattened, distended brockage from the obverse of a previously struck coin, indicating that this die cap probably produced counterbrockages before freeing itself from the obverse die. This piece is the most spectacular and dramatic Large Cent die cap known.

Rarity: Unique
Value: $75,000

4.

1898 Barber Quarter
Obverse Die Cap, Reverse Brockage—PCGS MS-62

This is the only obverse die cap known from the 1892-1916 Barber Quarter series, and the reverse is also significant due to the presence of a flat, distended brockage of the obverse design. Attractively toned, this piece is so deep that it barely fits into the PCGS holder in which it is mounted. Both error coin collectors and those that specialize in Barber coinage would benefit from including this important rarity in their numismatic collection.

Rarity: Unique
Value: $75,000

5.

1861 Indian Cent and Undated Indian Cent
Obverse and Reverse Die Caps—PCGS MS-64

Very few Indian Cent die caps are known even when we consider examples that are held individually in private collections. As a set, this obverse and reverse die cap pair is unique. Both examples are in near-Mint condition and would serve as a highlight in any specialized collection of U.S. Mint errors.

Rarity: Unique (as a Pair)
Value: $65,000

6.

1895-O Barber Dime
Obverse Die Cap—PCGS MS-64

For several reasons, this coin is one of the most significant errors featured in this book. First, the New Orleans Mint is one of the most challenging U.S. coinage facilities to represent in a collection of error coinage. Second, there are very few obverse die caps known from the entire Barber Dime series of 1892-1916. Finally, the 1895-O is a key-date issue with just 440,000 pieces struck for circulation.

Certified as a near-Gem by PCGS, this error features a deep die cap on a rare, key-date Barber Dime.

Rarity: Unique
Value: $50,000

7.

1865 Two-Cent Piece

Obverse Die Cap, Reverse Brockage—PCGS MS-64 Red and Brown

This spectacular 2¢ Die Cap is extremely rare and is so deep that it barely fits in the holder. It has a brockage on the reverse of the obverse design. The design has expanded considerably and the image of the shield covers almost the entire reverse. This die cap may have been struck from proof dies. This incredible obverse die cap is in Gem Mint State condition and was certified by PCGS.

Rarity: Unique
Value: $50,000

8.

1862 Indian Cent

Obverse Die Cap—PCGS MS-62

One of very few die caps known from the entire Indian Cent series of 1859-1909, this piece is of further significance because it is struck on a copper-nickel planchet from the early years of this design type. Although too deep to be certified, this die cap has been authenticated by PCGS and is accompanied by an insert. The surfaces exhibit equally pleasing technical quality and eye appeal, and the coin is in the Choice Mint State category.

Rarity: 7 Known
Value: $40,000

9.

1859 Indian Cent

Obverse Die Cap—NGC MS-61

There are only two obverse die caps reported for the 1859 Indian Cent, which is an important issue in its own right as a one-year type with the laurel wreath reverse. This dramatic error features a deep die cap with the rim of uniformly height around the entire circumference of the coin.

Rarity: 2 Known
Value: $40,000

10.

1855 Upright 55 Large Cent

Obverse Die Cap—NGC AU-58 Brown

Unique for an obverse die cap error on an 1855 Coronet Cent, this coin features a deep cap that nearly defies mounting in an NGC holder.

There are only a handful of die caps known from the entire United States Large Cent series. This important 1855 Upright 55 is nearly Mint State with glossy, problem-free surfaces.

Rarity: Unique
Value: $40,000

11.

Undated Copper-Nickel Indian Cent
Reverse Die Cap—NGC MS-66

The use of the oak wreath and shield reverse design attributes this reverse die cap error to 1860-1864. This is a very deep reverse die cap for a Copper-Nickel Indian Cent; most examples of this type that I have handled are actually quite shallow. Additionally, much of the definition in the obverse design is still visible, although the entire design on that side of the coin has become flat and distended from being struck into other planchets that were fed into the press after this piece capped the reverse die. Solidly graded as a Gem, this coin is a phenomenal example of a very rare U.S. Mint error.

Rarity: 3 Known
Value: $25,000

12.

1981-P Roosevelt Dime
Obverse Die Cap, Reverse Brockage Overstruck on a
Lincoln Cent Obverse Die Cap—MS-65 Brown

One of only two U.S. off-metal, dual denomination die caps known, this error is struck on a planchet intended for a 1981-P Lincoln Cent. Indeed, the planchet was first fed into a Cent press, where it became an obverse die cap. The cap appears to have struck several additional Cent planchets that caused it to curve up around the base of the die in a dramatic fashion. After finally ejecting from the Cent press, this piece then found its way into a Dime press where it once again became an obverse die cap, this time for a Roosevelt Dime die. The reverse acquired a brockage from a struck Roosevelt Dime that was still lying in the collar. Subsequent impressions while capping the Roosevelt Dime obverse die deepened the cap and all but obliterated the reverse brockage. A truly fascinating error, this piece offers keen insight into not only the minting process as a whole, but also the manner in which several different kinds of mint errors are created.

Rarity: Unique
Value: $25,000

13.

1999-P Susan B. Anthony Dollar
Reverse Die Cap—PCGS MS-65

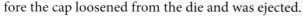

An important modern U.S. Mint error, this piece is the only reverse die cap reported for an Anthony Dollar. The bottle-cap shape that this error has assumed is uncommonly deep for a reverse die cap. The obverse design has expanded considerably creating brockages before the cap loosened from the die and was ejected.

Rarity: Unique
Value: $20,000

14.

1941 Jefferson Nickel
Mated Pair of a Reverse Die Cap and Reverse Full-Mirror Brockage—ANACS MS-63

This is the earliest known mated pair of Nickel errors that comprises a die cap and a brockage. The first example is a reverse die cap, and it is mated with another error that features a full mirror brockage on the reverse. The two coins fit snugly together, confirming that they are indeed a mated pair.

Rarity: Unique
Value: $12,500

15.

1999-P Pennsylvania Statehood Quarters
Mated Pair of Obverse Die Caps—As Struck

An extraordinary and seldom-encountered error, this mated pair started out being double struck. After the second impression, the planchet capped the obverse die, acquiring a deep cap as it was struck into several additional planchets. The final planchet struck by the die cap actually adhered itself to the cap and started to develop into a cap itself. Both caps fit snugly together, confirming that they actually capped the obverse die together for several strikes.

Rarity: Unique
Value: $12,500

16.

Philadelphia Mint Mercury Dime
Reverse Die Cap—PCGS MS-62

Although technically a reverse die cap, this error was struck in a press where the reverse was the hammer die and the obverse was the anvil die. This die cap features an incuse brockage of the reverse design on the obverse. Obviously, the cap was impressed into the reverse of a previously struck Mercury Dime. Although it is possible for struck coins to find their way back into the collar inverted, "flipped over" brockages occur much less frequently than those with the same orientation as properly struck coins from that press. The obverse brockage that this cap displays is flat and distended from having produced several counterbrockages.

This important error is unique for its type in the Mercury Dime series. Certified as Mint State by PCGS, this die cap would fit equally well into either a specialized error collection or an advanced set of Mercury Dimes.

Rarity: Unique
Value: $7,500

17.

1981-P Kennedy Half Dollar
Double-Struck Obverse Die Cap,
Reverse Brockage and Indent—MS-63

Struck twice, this planchet then capped the obverse die for many additional impressions. The reverse acquired an incuse brockage of the obverse design, most detail of which was subsequently lost through the creation of several counterbrockage errors. The reverse was struck into a blank planchet that partly overlaid another planchet that was properly seated in the collar. This impression indented the shape of the partially overlapping planchet into the reverse of this die cap. Truly an incredible error, the sides of the cap are so high that it will not fit into any of the holders currently in use by the major third-party certification services.

Rarity: 5 Known
Value: $5,000

18.

1976-D Bicentennial Kennedy Half Dollar
Obverse Die Cap, Reverse Brockage—PCGS MS-65

Obverse die caps that are as deep as this piece are seldom encountered in a Kennedy Half Dollar. When you consider that this error also occurred on an example of the short-lived Bicentennial type (produced solely in 1975 and 1976), the importance of this coin becomes even more obvious. The reverse is an incuse brockage that has become flat and distended from creating at least four or five counterbrockage errors. The outline of Kennedy's portrait is still visible in the brockage, however, as are the distended letters in the motto IN GOD WE TRUST.

Rarity: 5 Known
Value: $5,000

19.

Canada, 1979 Cent, KM-59.2

Reverse Die Cap Struck on a Quarter Planchet—As Struck

An almost unbelievable error, this coin is a reverse die cap of a 1979 Canadian Cent struck on a planchet intended for a Quarter. In this case, the reverse appears to have been used as the hammer die in the press, and it struck so many additional planchets that the cap has acquired a very high rim.

Wrong planchet errors are rare in their own right. The present example is even rarer because it also combines a second error in the form of the die cap.

Rarity: 2-3 Known
Value: $1,500

20.

1999-P Statehood Quarter

Double-Struck Obverse Die Cap, Reverse Brockage and
Double Indent—ANACS MS-65

A highly unusual error, the obverse die cap occurred first. It was followed by a reverse brockage that subsequently became flat and distended through the creation of several counterbrockage errors on different planchets. After freeing itself from the obverse die, the cap then rotated and received another impression from the obverse die that is approximately 50% off-center at 10-11 o'clock. The reverse also acquired two indented strikes, further obliterating the incuse brockage on that side of the coin. Since the reverse design is not present at all, I cannot identify this Statehood Quarter by type. The date 1999 is barely discernible as part of the reverse brockage, however, and the obverse clearly shows the P mintmark. The U.S. Mint struck five different Statehood Quarters in 1999, so this error must be an example of the Delaware, Pennsylvania, New Jersey, Georgia or Connecticut types.

Rarity: 10 Known
Value: $1,500

21.

1985-P Roosevelt Dime

Obverse Die Cap—MS-65

This obverse die cap on a Roosevelt Dime is quite deep. The coin obviously capped the die for at least four or five subsequent strikes because the reverse design has become extremely flat and distorted. A dramatic modern error, this piece was discovered shortly after escaping the Philadelphia Mint and has survived in Gem Mint State.

Rarity: 20 Known
Value: $500

Price Guide for Die Caps

Denomination	Obverse Cap XF	Obverse Cap Unc	Reverse Cap XF	Reverse Cap Unc
Large Cent	$30,000	$75,000	–	–
Indian Cent 1859	$20,000	$60,000	–	–
Indian Cent 1860-1864	$15,000	$50,000	$10,000	$20,000
Indian Cent 1864-1909	$15,000	$50,000	$7,500	$15,000
Lincoln Cent 1943 Steel	–	–	–	–
Lincoln Cent Wheat Ears	$1,000	$2,500	$500	$1,000
Lincoln Cent Memorial	$150	$200	$50	$100
2 Cent Piece	$20,000	$50,000	$15,000	$30,000
3 Cent Nickel	–	–	–	–
Shield Nickel	–	–	–	–
Liberty Nickel	$12,500	$25,000	–	–
Buffalo Nickel (1 Known)	–	$30,000	–	–
Jefferson Nickel War Time	$10,000	–	–	–
Jefferson Nickel	$200	$350	$150	$250
Barber Dime	$25,000	$30,000	$17,500	$20,000
Mercury Dime (2 Known)	$5,000	$7,500	–	–
Roosevelt Dime Silver	$750	$1,250	$500	$750
Roosevelt Dime Clad	$200	$400	$200	$250
Barber Quarter	$30,000	$75,000	–	–
Washington Quarter Silver	$1,500	$4,000	$1,500	$2,000
Washington Quarter Clad	$350	$750	$250	$350
State Quarter	N/A	$1,000	N/A	$600
Kennedy Half Silver	$3,000	$5,000	$2,000	$3,000
Kennedy Half Clad	$2,000	$3,500	$1,500	$2,000
Kennedy Half Bicentennial	$2,500	$4,000	$1,750	$2,500
Eisenhower Dollar	–	$30,000	–	–
Susan B Anthony Dollar	N/A	$20,000	N/A	$15,000
Sacagawea Dollar	N/A	$20,000	N/A	$15,000

Chapter 7

Double and Multiple Strikes

*W*hen a blank planchet is struck by the dies, the normal procedure is for the feeders to eject the struck coin out of the collar and into a chute. If there is a malfunction and the struck coin is not ejected, it may receive a second, third and possibly even more strikes from the dies. Double and multiple struck coins can also be found in combination with many other types of errors and are often very dramatic.

1.

1904 Liberty Double Eagle

Double Struck—PCGS MS-63

PCGS has described this unique 1904 Double Eagle error as being double struck. Close examination with a loupe reveals the two impressions on the obverse at Liberty's portrait, the stars, date and denticles. This feature is also present on the reverse, but only at select portions of the eagle, shield and denticles. The coin rotated only slightly between strikes, so the spread is not all that wide. Had the doubling been more dramatic, this error would almost certainly have been spotted in the Mint and the coin would have been destroyed.

Rarity: Unique
Value: $102,500

2.

Undated Philadelphia Mint Morgan Silver Dollar

Double Struck—PCGS AU-58

Only 10 double-struck errors are known from the entire Morgan Dollar series, and this undated example from the Philadelphia Mint is by far the most dramatic. The second strike is 40% off-center and positioned exactly at 6 o'clock. There are two portraits visible on the obverse, and two eagles are present on the reverse. The second strike, however, was positioned in such a way that the date is off the planchet, and it also obliterated the date from the first strike. The AU-58 grade assigned by PCGS confirms that this error was discovered shortly after leaving the Mint and has since been carefully preserved in numismatic circles.

Rarity: 10 Known
Value: $100,000

3.

1853 United States Assay Office of Gold, $20 Gold, 900 THOUS, K-18, Rarity-2 (as a Type)

Double Struck—NGC AU-55

Both the obverse and the reverse of this 1853 Assay Office $20 are double struck, the reverse with slightly more spread between the impressions than the obverse. This coin would still be a highly desirable representative of the type even if it were not a major error. There is considerable luster remaining, and the color is a richly original, green-gold shade.

Major mint errors on federal gold coins are extremely rare, while those on Private and Territorial gold coins are all but known. This incredible double-struck Assay Office $20 would serve as a centerpiece in an advanced Territorial gold collection, a set built around major gold coin errors or a more general collection of United States and related gold coinage.

Rarity: Unique
Value: $75,000

4.

Proof 1887 Three-Dollar Gold Piece
Triple Struck—PCGS Proof-63 Cameo

This proof 1887 Three-Dollar gold piece is triple struck with the third strike rotated 165 degrees. There is considerable detail remaining from the first strike, particularly on the reverse. A very rare error, this coin is also significant due to the rarity of the proof 1887 Three-Dollar as an issue.

Rarity: 4 Known
Value: $60,000

5.

1924 Standing Liberty Quarter
Double Struck, Obverse Indent—ANACS AU-55

All Standing Liberty Quarter errors are rare and eagerly sought by specialists. This 1924 is double struck on the reverse with the second impression approximately 20% off-center between 11 and 12 o'clock. As a result, two eagles are visible on that side of the coin. The obverse, on the other hand, was indented by a blank planchet during the second strike. The definition within the indent is somewhat flat and distended, although all major design elements are still readily evident.

There are just three double-struck Standing Liberty Quarters known, and this piece is the only one that is also an example of an indent error. It would serve as a highlight in either a collection of major mint errors or an advanced set of Standing Liberty Quarters.

Rarity: 3 Known
Value: $60,000

6.

1800 Draped Bust Silver Dollar
Double Struck—PCGS XF-45

This Draped Bust Dollar is double struck with the second strike 15% off-center at 9 o'clock. A very dramatic Mint error, much of the detail from the first strike is still present.

This is one of the most spectacular early U.S. Mint errors that I have ever encountered. While a handful of double-struck Draped Bust Dollars are known, most are either slightly rotated in the collar with little definition remaining from the first strike, or are so worn that it is difficult to appreciate the error. With the second strike so far off-center and the surfaces in a relatively high level of preservation, this double-struck 1800 Bust Dollar is unique.

Rarity: 5 Known
Value: $50,000

7.

1890 Seated Dime
Double Struck—PCGS MS-62

After being struck once and partially ejected from the press, this 1890 Seated Dime rotated 90 degrees counterclockwise and received a second strike that is 75% off-center at 7 o'clock. The date from the first strike is still clear, and the second impression is also die struck on the reverse.

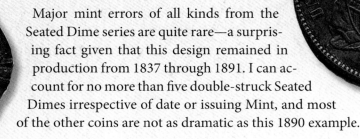

Major mint errors of all kinds from the Seated Dime series are quite rare—a surprising fact given that this design remained in production from 1837 through 1891. I can account for no more than five double-struck Seated Dimes irrespective of date or issuing Mint, and most of the other coins are not as dramatic as this 1890 example.

Rarity: 5 Known
Value: $25,000

8.

1921 Morgan Silver Dollar
Double Struck—NGC MS-60

Although double struck in the collar with only slight rotation between strikes, there is distinct separation between the two impressions. The doubling is most readily evident at the borders and on the edge, where there are two sets of denticles and two sets of reeding, respectively. Only one other Morgan Dollar error displays two sets of reeding from having been double struck in the collar, and that coin is also a 1921 that ANACS has certified as MS-64.

Rarity: 10 Known
Value: $10,000

9.

1652 Massachusetts Bay Colony, Pine Tree Shilling, Small Planchet, Noe-29, Rarity-3 (as a Die Pair)
Flipover Double Struck—PCGS VF-30

Among the earliest coins struck in the New World, the Pine Tree issues of 1667-1682 were the culmination of a coinage system introduced by the Massachusetts Bay Colony in 1652. These coins were struck in Threepence, Sixpence and Shilling (or Twelvepence) denominations using silver bullion from the West Indies. The coinage facility was located in Boston.

One of the later Pine Tree Shillings produced, this coin was prepared on a small planchet. It is a flipover double-strike error. In other words, the coin was first struck properly but then found its way back into the press upside down, after which it was struck a second time. With much of the detail still showing from the first strike, this is a very rare error from the Colonial era of American history.

Rarity: 5 Known
Value: $7,500

10.

1918 Standing Liberty Quarter
Double Struck—NGC AU-58 Full Head

Double struck in the collar, this early-date Standing Liberty Quarter shows two distinct sets of reeding around the edge as well as two rims on each side. This 1918 Standing Liberty Quarter was double struck in the collar and shows two distinct sets of reeding and edges.

This 1918 is the highest-graded example of the three double-struck Standing Liberty Quarters known.

Rarity: 3 Known
Value: $7,500

11.

1941 Mercury Dime
Triple Struck—ANACS MS-60

This triple-struck Mercury Dime error features three distinct sets of the motto IN GOD WE TRUST, the truncation of Liberty's neck and the digits in the date. Much of the other definition from the first two strikes has been obliterated.

A strictly Uncirculated example, both sides are adorned with subtle golden-brown toning that enhances already impressive eye appeal.

Rarity: Unique
Value: $7,500

12.

Undated Denver Mint Mercury Dime
Double Struck—PCGS XF-45

The second strike is 25% off-center at 7 o'clock, an impressive error that has yielded a Mercury Dime with no date. The D mintmark from the first strike, however, is still clear at the lower-left reverse border. Die struck on both sides, portions of Liberty's portrait and the reverse fasces from the first strike are still readily evident.

Rarity: 4 Known
Value: $7,500

13.

2000-P Sacagawea Dollar
Multi-Struck—ANACS MS-63

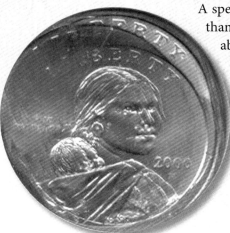

A spectacular modern mint error, this 2000-P Sacagawea Dollar is struck no less than 15 times. The coin rotated only slightly between strikes, although considerable detail remains from many of the impressions on both the obverse and the reverse. The surfaces are free of wear and other signs of significant handling, and the coin is solidly graded as Choice Mint State.

Rarity: 3 Known
Value: $5,000

14.

1865 Three-Cent Nickel
Flipover Double Struck—NGC MS-61

Both sides of this coin retain considerable portions of the first strike.

This is a dramatic error when encountered on any coin type. This particular example is a Three-Cent Nickel—a short-lived denomination that is not known for having produced many errors of any type.

Rarity: 2 Known
Value: $5,000

15.

Undated Philadelphia Mint Liberty Nickel
Double Struck—ICG MS-64

This double-struck Liberty Nickel has a second strike that is 70% off-center between 6 and 7 o'clock, the dies having struck both sides on the second impression. The off-center second strike caused the planchet to expand considerably in size, and it also obliterated the date area from the first strike. The word CENTS is included as part of the reverse design, so this Liberty Nickel error could have been struck anytime from 1883 through the series' end in 1912.

Rarity: 5 Known
Value: $5,000

16.

Undated Denver Mint Eisenhower Dollar

Double Struck—ANACS MS-64

Die struck on both sides, this impressive Eisenhower Dollar displays a second impression that is 15-20% off-center at 5-6 o'clock. The word LIBERTY appears twice on the obverse, as does the denomination ONE DOLLAR on the reverse.

Double-struck Eisenhower Dollars are very scarce coins that enjoy strong demand among error coin specialists. The brevity of the Eisenhower Dollar series (1971-1978) and the large size of these coins explain why so few double-struck errors of this type have been discovered.

Rarity: 20 Known
Value: $5,000

17.

1969 Lincoln Cent

Double Struck on a Canada, 10 Cents Planchet—NGC MS-62

A major mint error that combines two blunders in the coining process, the first mistake came when a planchet intended for a Canadian Dime found its way into a Lincoln Cent press. The coin was then struck twice by the Lincoln Cent dies, the planchet rotating several degrees in the collar between impressions.

In 1968 and 1969, the Philadelphia Mint was tasked with producing Dimes for Canada alongside its regular duty of striking coins for the United States. There are only a few U.S. error coins of all kinds that were accidentally struck on Canadian Dime planchets during those two years.

Rarity: 3 Known
Value: $5,000

18.

Proof 1968-S Jefferson Nickel
Double Struck Die Trial—ICG Proof-65

The extreme lack of detail confirms the first error as a die adjustment. The coin is also double struck in the collar, and it rotated 90 degrees between impressions. This piece may have been a die trial for the striking of proof 1968-S Jefferson Nickels. On the other hand, it could have been struck under circumstances where a mechanical or other malfunction caused the press to loose pressure. Either way, this coin is unique for a proof Jefferson Nickel with this interesting combination of minting errors.

Rarity: Unique
Value: $5,000

19.

1972-D Eisenhower Dollar
Double Struck—ANACS MS-63

The second strike is rotated 90 degrees in relation to the first and, since it occurred outside of the collar, the coin is now also broadstruck. Details from the first strike are discernible at the upper-obverse and lower-reverse borders.

Rarity: 20 Known
Value: $4,000

20.

German States, Frankfurt, Undated 2 Talers, Dav-651

Double Struck—MS-62

The second strike has effaced the date area at the lower reverse so it is not possible to determine whether this piece was struck in 1860, 1861, 1862 or 1866. The second strike is 80% off-center at 5 o'clock, and it is also uniface with the reverse blank.

Although many Austrian and German States Talers were struck twice to bring out the maximum amount of detail from the dies, this Frankfurt piece is a true error since the second strike is off-center.

Rarity: Unique
Value: $3,000

21.

Mexico, 1955 Restrike 5 Pesos, Fr-168R

Double Struck—ANACS MS-63

This Mexican gold 5 Pesos was double struck in the collar, the coin rotating considerably between impressions. Much of the detail from the first strike still readily evident.

Although Mexican errors in non-gold denominations are encountered relatively often in the numismatic market, major mint errors on gold coins are exceedingly rare.

Rarity: Unique
Value: $2,500

Price Guide for Double and Multiple Strikes

Denomination	XF/AU	Unc
Large Cent	$1,000	$7,500
Indian Cent	$600	$1,000
Lincoln Cent 1930 and Earlier	$850	$1,500
Lincoln Cent 1943 Steel	$400	$1,500
Proof Lincoln Cent	N/A	$4,000
3 Cent Nickel	$2,000	$3,500
Liberty Nickel	$4,000	$10,000
Buffalo Nickel	$5,000	$10,000
Jefferson Nickel War Time	$750	$2,000
Proof Jefferson Nickel	N/A	$6,000
Barber Dime	$4,000	$10,000
Mercury Dime	$3,500	$8,500
Proof Clad Dime	N/A	$6,000
Standing Liberty Quarter	$15,000	$50,000
Washington Quarter Silver	$200	$350
State Quarter	N/A	$350 – $750
Proof Clad Quarter	N/A	$7,500
Walking Liberty Half	$10,000	$25,000
Franklin Half	$5,000	$10,000
Kennedy Half Silver	$1,500	$2,500
Kennedy Half Clad	N/A	$750
Proof Kennedy Half Clad	N/A	$7,500
Morgan Dollar	$12,500	$25,000
Peace Dollar	$15,000	$50,000
Eisenhower Dollar	$2,000	$3,000
Susan B Anthony Dollar	N/A	$1,000 – $2,500
Sacagawea Dollar	N/A	$1,500 – $3,000

O verstrikes are coins that have been struck over a previously struck coin of a different type and/or denomination. Generally speaking, there are two different types of overstrikes. The first type is a Double Denomination that involves two denominations of coins from the same country. An example from the United States is a Lincoln Cent overstruck on a Roosevelt Dime. Such errors are known on many denominations of coins from many countries.

The other type of overstrike is an error that involves a coin overstruck on another coin from a different era or country. Overstrikes of this type can be the result of a genuine Mint error or a deliberate overstriking either for official or unofficial purposes. In ancient times, it was not uncommon to strike coins over previously struck coins with portraits of earlier rulers. In Colonial times, coins were sometimes taken from circulation and overstruck using another coin design, regardless of whether the two types were from the same country origin.

1.

1859 Indian Cent
Overstruck on an 1857 Seated Half Dime—PCGS MS-63

This double-denomination coin is one of the most significant mint errors ever discovered, and it has been well documented in numismatic circles for decades. The obverse of an 1857 Seated Half Dime was overstruck with an obverse die for the 1859 Indian Cent. The reverse of the Half Dime is unaffected by the error. The error is so dramatic that it may have been deliberately prepared by someone in the Philadelphia Mint, although I have been unable to find any evidence that positively confirms or refutes this possibility.

Rarity: Unique
Value: $100,000

2.

2000-P Jefferson Nickel
Overstruck on a 1978-D Lincoln Cent—ANACS MS-64 Red and Brown

A major error, this 2000-P Jefferson Nickel was overstruck on a 1978-D Lincoln Cent. Considerable detail from the Cent undertype is still clearly visible, particularly on the reverse. How a double-denomination error struck in two different coinage facilities from dies dated 22 years apart could have been produced is anyone's guess. Regardless of how it came into being, this coin ranks as one of the most important major mint errors of the early 21st century.

Rarity: Unique
Value: $20,000

3.

1951 Roosevelt Dime
Overstruck on a Honduras, 1956 Centavo, KM-77.2—ANACS MS-61 Brown

The United States Mint routinely strikes coins for other countries. This 1956 Roosevelt Dime was overstruck on a Honduran copper Centavo in the Philadelphia Mint. The undertype is difficult to discern, but traces of the Centavo design are visible if you look closely enough.

All dual-denomination errors involving a Dime struck over a different coin are extremely rare since the planchet being fed into the press must be no larger than 17.9 millimeters (the diameter of the United States Dime since about 1829) in order to fit in the collar.

Rarity: 3 Known
Value: $7,500

4.

1941 Washington Quarter
Overstruck on a Lincoln Cent of the Wheat Ears Reverse Type—
ANACS MS-64 Brown

This is the earliest-dated, double-denomination Washington Quarter error. It is a 1941 Quarter struck over a struck Lincoln Cent of the Wheat Ears Reverse type. The undertype no longer displays the date, but the Wheat Ears Reverse confirms that the Cent was struck sometime between 1909 and 1941. The error is also a flipover because you can see remnants of the Lincoln Cent reverse on the obverse of the Washington Quarter.

The ANACS holder in which this coin is encapsulated makes it difficult to discern the date, but most of the 4 and part of the second 1 are visible from the Washington Quarter obverse die. An attractive near-Gem, both sides have a 50-50 mix of blended orange-red luster and medium-brown patina.

Rarity: Unique
Value: $6,000

5.

1951 Roosevelt Dime
Overstruck on a Costa Rica, 1951 5 Centimos, KM-184.1—ANACS MS-63

Seven million examples of the Costa Rica 5 Centimos of the KM-184.1 variety were struck in the United States Mint in Philadelphia during 1951. Apparently, one of those coins remained in a tote bin that was subsequently filled with U.S. Dime planchets. When the planchets were fed into the Dime press, this Costa Rica 5 Centimos worked itself loose from the inside of the tote and also found its way into the press. This dual-denomination error is also a flipover as remnants of the reverse design of the 5 Centimos type are intermingled with the devices on the obverse of the Roosevelt Dime.

Rarity: 2 Known
Value: $6,000

6.

1964 Washington Quarter
Overstruck on a Lincoln Cent of the Memorial Reverse Type— ANACS MS-64 Red and Brown

A full date is present as part of the obverse design of the Washington Quarter, and a considerable amount of detail from the Lincoln Cent is also noted. Double-denomination errors from the Washington Quarter series are genuinely rare coins. The present off-metal example is an attractive near-Gem with appreciable mint-red luster remaining.

Rarity: 10-15 Known
Value: $5,000

7.

2000-P Sacagawea Dollar
Overstruck on a 2000 Maryland Statehood Quarter—PCGS MS-64

A flipover double-denomination error, the obverse of the Sacagawea is overstruck on the reverse of the Statehood Quarter, and vice versa. This is a beautiful and highly desirable near-Gem with full luster and no significant distractions.

Rarity: 20 Known
Value: $5,000

8.

1953-S Washington Quarter
Overstruck on a 1953-S Jefferson Nickel—ANACS AU-58

A fascinating and rare "30-Cent" piece, most dual-denomination errors coins occur in the fictitious denominations of Six Cents (involving a Cent and a Nickel) and 11 Cents (involving a Cent and a Dime). Nearly in the Mint State category, this minimally circulated example includes bold definition to the date and S mintmark as part of the Washington Quarter design.

Rarity: 10-15 Known
Value: $5,000

Price Guide for Double Denominations

Denomination	Struck On	Circulated	AU	Unc
Lincoln Cent Wheat Ears	Mercury Dime	$6,000	$12,500	$20,000
Lincoln Cent Wheat Ears	Roosevelt Dime	$4,000	$5,000	$6,000
Lincoln Cent Wheat Ears	Foreign Coin	$2,000	$2,500	–
Lincoln Cent Memorial	Roosevelt Dime Silver	$3,000	$4,500	$6,000
Lincoln Cent Memorial	Roosevelt Dime Clad	N/A	N/A	$750
Lincoln Cent Memorial	Foreign Coin	N/A	$600	$750
Jefferson Nickel	Lincoln Cent Wheat Ears	$1,500	$2,000	$2,500
Jefferson Nickel	Lincoln Cent Memorial	N/A	$750	$1,000
Jefferson Nickel	Foreign Coin	$1,000	$1,250	$1,500
Jefferson Nickel	Roosevelt Dime	$1,000	$1,250	$1,500
Roosevelt Dime Silver	Foreign Coin	$4,000	$5,000	$7,500
Roosevelt Dime Clad	Foreign Coin	$3,000	$4,000	$5,000
Washington Quarter Silver	Lincoln Cent Wheat Ears	$3,000	$4,000	$6,000
Washington Quarter Silver	Lincoln Cent Memorial	$2,500	$3,000	$3,500
Washington Quarter Silver	Foreign Coin	$2,500	$3,000	$3,500
Washington Quarter Silver	Jefferson Nickel	$3,000	$4,000	$6,000
Washington Quarter Silver	Roosevelt Dime Silver	$2,500	$3,000	$3,500
Washington Quarter Clad	Lincoln Cent Memorial	$2,500	$3,000	$3,500
Washington Quarter Clad	Foreign Coin	$2,000	$2,500	$3,000
Washington Quarter Clad	Jefferson Nickel	$2,500	$3,000	$3,500
Washington Quarter Clad	Roosevelt Dime Clad	$2,000	$2,500	$3,000
State Quarter	Jefferson Nickel	N/A	$7,500	$10,000
State Quarter (Extremely Rare)	Any Other Denomination	N/A	$10,000	$12,500
Franklin Half	Lincoln Cent Wheat Ears	$7,500	$12,500	$20,000
Kennedy Half (Extremely Rare)	Any Denomination	$7,500	$10,000	$12,500
Eisenhower Dollar (Extremely Rare)	Any Denomination	–	–	–
Sacagawea Dollar	Maryland State Quarter	N/A	$3,000	$4,000

Chapter 9
Experimental Strikes

*T*here are approximately 20 known 1999 State Quarters struck on Experimental Planchets. All five states in the 1999 series (DE, PA, CT, GA and NJ) have been discovered. These Experimental State Quarters have sold for as high as $10,000 each, depending on which state, the coin's condition and which type of experimental composition was used. There are four known types of experimental compositions which have been discovered so far on 1999 State Quarters that vary in color and whether or not they have a copper center core. These coins were analyzed by spectroscopy (SEM-EDX) using electron microscopy and energy-dispersive x-rays to determine the alloy composition. The predominant metal is copper, followed by zinc. There are also small percentages of manganese and nickel. PCGS and NGC have both authenticated and certified these 1999 State Quarters as being struck on experimental planchets. There is only one 2000 dated State Quarter struck on an experimental planchet known, and is valued at $25,000.

1.

2000-P Massachusetts Statehood Quarter
Struck on an Experimental Planchet—PCGS MS-65

This Massachusetts piece is the only 2000-dated Statehood Quarter known to have been struck on an experimental planchet in error.

The planchet upon which error is struck was undoubtedly leftover from 1999, when the U.S. Mint conducted a series of tests to determine a suitably alloy for the Sacagawea Dollar.

Rarity: Unique
Value: $25,000

2.

1999-P Susan B. Anthony Dollar
Struck on an Experimental Planchet—PCGS MS-67

Four Anthony Dollars are known struck on experimental planchets designed to test proposed alloys for the Sacagawea Dollar introduced in 2000. One of these errors has the same color as the regular-issue Sacagawea Dollar, but it does not have a copper core at its center. The example pictured here has a slight greenish color to the surfaces and includes a copper-center core. The final piece of which I have specific knowledge also has a greenish color to the surfaces, but it is missing the copper-center core.

These experimental planchets are also known to have produced wrong metal errors on 1999 and 2000-dated Statehood Quarters, a few of which are pictured above.

Rarity: 4 Known
Value: $17,500

3.

1999-P New Jersey Statehood Quarter
Struck on an Experimental Planchet—PCGS MS-66

As with the 1999-P Delaware Quarter above, this New Jersey example was mistakenly struck on a planchet that was intended for use in the testing process that preceded selection of a suitable alloy for the Sacagawea Dollar.

Rarity: 2 Known
Value: $10,000

4.

1999-P Delaware Statehood Quarter
Struck on an Experimental Planchet—PCGS MS-66

Statehood Quarters struck on experimental planchets in error are known in four different compositions. The different types vary in surface color and whether or not they include a copper-center core. It appears that all four planchet types were initially prepared to test possible alloys for the Sacagawea Dollar that the Mint introduced in 2000. A few of those planchets, however, found their way into presses that were striking regular-issue of other types or denominations.

Rarity: 5 Known
Value: $7,500

Price Guide for Experimental Strikes

Prices fluctuate due to the date, grade, eye appeal and how dramatic the striking error is. Rarity is also a factor. The price is sometimes based on the rarity and grade of the type of coin as well as how rare the error is. There is no price guide for this chapter because of the extreme rarity and low number of errors available.

Chapter 10

Feeder Finger Strikes

After a recent tour of the U.S. Mint in Philadelphia, it was discovered that the minting process had changed to some degree. One of the changes was that "feeder fingers" were used during the striking of all denominations of U.S. coins. Prior to this tour, U.S. coins that were struck on feeder finger tips were authenticated and described as being struck on aluminum scrap. Coins from all modern denominations have been discovered that were struck on the tips of these feeder fingers.

1.

2000-P Sacagawea Dollar
Struck on Feeder Finger Tip—PCGS MS-65

The strike is quite nicely centered on the feeder finger tip, and there is considerable detail on both sides of the "coin." Of particular note in this regard are the date and mintmark on the obverse, both of which are clearly visible.

Feeder finger strike errors have been discovered for all denominations being produced in the modern United States Mint. Most examples, however, display far less definition of the coin's design than this Sacagawea Dollar.

Rarity: 5 Known
Value: $10,000

2.

Undated (2000) South Carolina Statehood Quarter

Multi-Struck on Feeder Finger Tip—ANACS MS-62

This broken piece of a feeder finger tip is struck no less than 14 times by the obverse and reverse dies of a 2000 South Carolina Quarter. Each individual strike is lined up right next to the previous strike, and all are discernible on both the obverse and the reverse. Unfortunately, there is no mintmark present so I cannot tell whether this spectacular error was struck in the Philadelphia Mint or the Denver Mint.

Rarity: 5 Known
Value: $7,500

3.

1998-P Washington Quarter

Struck on Feeder Finger Tip—ANACS MS-64

The portion of the feeder finger tip on which this error is struck is nearly large enough to display all portions of the obverse and reverse designs. In fact, only a small portion of the Washington Quarter design is missing at the upper-left obverse and the lower-left reverse borders.

Rarity: 2 Known
Value: $7,500

4.

Undated (1999) Connecticut Statehood Quarter

Multi-Struck on Feeder Finger Tip—NGC MS-65

This Connecticut Statehood Quarter is multi-struck on a feeder finger tip. The error is even more dramatic because it is struck multiple times, each impression being off-center with the result that portions of the actual feeder finger tip are included alongside the obverse and reverse designs. Most feeder finger strikes are better centered than this piece and, as such, do not show any portion of a blank feeder finger tip. The mintmark position on the obverse is off the tip, with the result that I cannot attribute this important error to either the Philadelphia or Denver Mint

Rarity: 5 Known
Value: $7,500

5.

Undated (2001) New York Statehood Quarter

Multi-Struck on Feeder Finger Tip—NGC MS-65

Another impressive example of this error type, this New York Statehood Quarter is multi-struck off-center on the feeder finger tip with the result that part of the actual feeder finger tip has survived intact.

Rarity: 3 Known
Value: $7,500

85

6.

2000-P Sacagawea Dollar
Triple-Struck on Feeder Finger Tip—PCGS MS-65

This error coin is triple struck on an aluminum feeder finger tip.

Although portions of the obverse and reverse designs are off the tip, and the tip has been completely obliterated by the strike, this piece is still one of the more desirable feeder finger strikes on a Sacagawea Dollar. Both sides are free of spotting and discoloration, which are distracting features that almost always accompany Sacagawea Dollar errors of this type.

Rarity: 5 Known
Value: $7,500

7.

2001-P New York Statehood Quarter
Triple-Struck on Feeder Finger Tip—PCGS MS-65

All three impressions are off-center, and a portion of the actual feeder finger tip has survived. There is also quite a bit of detail to the obverse and reverse designs, and it includes and discernible P mintmark.

Rarity: 5 Known
Value: $7,500

8.

Chile, 1998 10 Pesos, KM-228.2

Double Struck on Feeder Finger—As Struck

An amazing error, this 1998 Chilean 10 Pesos coin is double struck on the actual feeder finger.

Most coins that are struck on feeder fingers break off, leaving us with only the tip. The discovery of this fully intact error is a major find in the error coin market of the 21st century.

Rarity: 5 Known
Value: $5,000

Price Guide for Feeder Finger Strikes

Denomination	Small	Medium	Large
Lincoln Cent Memorial	$2,500	$3,500	$6,000
Jefferson Nickel	$3,000	$4,500	$6,000
Roosevelt Dime Clad	$3,000	$6,000	$7,500
Washington Quarter Clad	$4,000	$6,000	$7,500
State Quarter	$4,500	$6,500	$8,500
Kennedy Half Clad	–	–	–
Susan B Anthony Dollar	–	–	$15,000
Sacagawea Dollar	$4,500	$7,500	$12,500

Chapter 11

Fold-Over Strikes

A folded, or fold-over strike, is one of the most dramatic types of errors. It occurs when a planchet is struck while standing vertically on its edge between the dies. The pressure imparted during the striking process is so great that it causes the planchet to bend and fold over.

Fold-overs can be on-center or off-center, and they come in many different shapes. There are a few fold-overs that are also examples of other types of errors. Fold-overs are rarely encountered on planchets larger than those intended for Quarters.

1.

Undated (1999) Connecticut Statehood Quarter

Fold-Over—As Struck

This is the only fold-over error known on a Connecticut Statehood Quarter, and it is also one of only two fold-over errors discovered from the entire Statehood Quarter series. Only the left obverse and the corresponding portion of the reverse were struck on the planchet, and portions of the words UNIT-ED and LIBERTY are struck over the fold on the obverse.

Although fold-over errors are known for all denominations from the Cent through the Half Dollar, most examples are Cents. Quarter and Half Dollar fold-overs are particularly elusive, and they are seldom present in even the most extensive error coin collections.

Rarity: Unique
Value: $7,500

2.

1999 Lincoln Cent
Multi-Struck Fold-over—ANACS MS-63 Red

Folded over three times and struck five times, the planchet has expanded to approximately the size of a Half Dollar. Quite a bit of detail is evident from at least one of the obverse impressions, including the date. This is one of the most intriguing fold-over errors that I have seen.

Rarity: Unique
Value: $2,000

3.

1981 Lincoln Cent
Fold-over—ANACS MS-63

Lincoln's portrait, the word LIBERTY and the date are all clear on the obverse. The reverse has even more definition, and only the denomination ONE CENT is off the planchet.

One of the earlier fold-over errors from the Lincoln Cent series that I have handled, this 1981 example is struck on a bronze planchet as opposed to a copper-plated zinc planchet as introduced in 1982.

Rarity: 20-50 Known
Value: $1,500

4.

Undated Lincoln Cent, Memorial Reverse Type
Fold-over—PCGS MS-65 Red

The planchet was horizontal when the dies came together, and it folded into this dramatic error. The planchet also expanded in size as a result of the error.

Rarity: 20-50 Known
Value: $1,000

Price Guide for Fold-Over Strikes

Denomination	AU	AU Dated	UNC	UNC Dated
Lincoln Cent Memorial Copper	$1,000	$1,250	$1,250	$1,500
Lincoln Cent Memorial Zinc	$750	$1,000	$1,000	$1,250
Jefferson Nickel	$2,500	$3,000	$3,000	$4,000
Roosevelt Dime Silver	$4,000	$5,000	$5,000	$6,000
Roosevelt Dime Clad	$3,000	$3,500	$3,500	$4,500
Washington Quarter Silver	$4,000	$5,000	$5,000	$10,000
Washington Quarter Clad	$3,500	$4,000	$4,000	$5,000
State Quarter	$4,000	$5,000	$5,000	$7,500

Chapter 12

Gold Errors

Other than a few known U.S. Mules, major errors on U.S. Gold coins are the most prized category of all mint errors. Gold errors are very rare and a few have traded in the $75,000 to $150,000 range. Even a broadstruck U.S. Gold coin can easily sell for $15,000 to $40,000 compared to a broadstruck Cent, Nickel, Dime or Quarter which all sell for well under $10. Many serious collectors of Gold Errors have to wait patiently for months and sometimes even years to acquire that one special piece for their collection. World Gold errors are highly coveted and just as rare as their U.S. counterparts. Despite this, they are undervalued, selling for a fraction of the price.

1.

1866 Liberty Quarter Eagle
Struck on a Three-Cent Nickel Planchet—NGC MS-66

The similarity in diameter between these two coin types (17.9 millimeters and 18 millimeters, respectively) allowed this Three-Cent Nickel planchet to fit nicely into the collar in a Liberty Quarter Eagle press. The planchet did not completely fill the press, however, and the impression is drawn ever-so-slightly toward the upper-right obverse and lower-left reverse borders. All design elements from the Quarter Eagle dies are present, nonetheless, and the overall definition is quite sharp.

An important discovery piece, this wrong planchet error on an 1866 Liberty Quarter Eagle was authenticated and certified by NGC in 2007. This piece is one of only two wrong planchet errors in the entire United States gold coin series that are listed at the major third-party certification services (PCGS and NGC). The other example is an 1851 Liberty Double Eagle struck on a Cent planchet that has also been authenticated and certified by NGC.

In addition to its status as a unique error on a 19th century U.S. gold coin, this piece is significant because the 1866 is a low-mintage issues with just 3,080 business strikes produced. It is one of the leading rarities in the regular-issue Liberty Quarter Eagle series of 1840-1907.

Rarity: Unique
Value: $250,000

2.

1806 Capped Bust Right Half Eagle, Pointed 6, Stars 8x5, BD-3, HBCC-3098, Rarity-7 (as a Die Pair)

Triple Struck—PCGS AU-50

The coin was first struck 10-15% off-center in normal alignment. It then rotated 90 degrees and was struck a second time properly centered between the dies. A third strike occurred after the coin rotated again, although this time the rotation was minimal.

This coin is pictured on the front cover of *Mint Error News Magazine*, Issue 16, Winter 2006. It is the earliest die state known for the extremely rare 1806 BD-3 Half Eagle variety. The stress caused by the striking of this error severely damaged the obverse die, which was in the anvil position in the press. A field break developed behind Liberty's head, as did a crack from stars 6-8. Very few additional coins were struck from this die pair before it was retired. Indeed, only six-to-ten examples of the 1806 BD-3 Half Eagle are believed to have survived. With the exception of this remarkable error, all known examples struck from this die pair display the aforementioned cracks on the obverse.

Rarity: Unique
Value: $150,000

3.

1804 Capped Bust Right Quarter Eagle, 14-Star Reverse, BD-2, HBCC-3011, Rarity-4 (as a Die Pair)

Double Struck—NGC Fine-15

The first strike is off-center, but the second is well centered on the planchet. The coin has acquired considerable wear, which could mean that the error was overlooked for many years. On the other hand, most pre-1834 United States gold coins remained in vaults as bank reserves, and it is unusual to find an example that grades less than XF-40. At the Fine grade level, this coin may have been identified as an error by a contemporary bank teller or bullion dealer who then carried it as a pocket piece for many years, thereby explaining the considerable wear that is present on both sides. Regardless of which of these theories is true, this remarkable piece remained unknown to the general numismatic market until the early 21st century. Today, it ranks as one of the most important U.S. gold coin errors of any type.

There are fewer than a dozen double-struck United States gold coins known, a total that includes all types from the Gold Dollar through the Double Eagle. This 1804 Quarter Eagle is of even further importance as an example of the first major design that the U.S. Mint used on a coin of this denomination.

As an issue, the 1804 has an estimated mintage of just 3,327 pieces. Fewer than 3,000 of those coins are believed to have been struck using the 14-Star reverse die.

Rarity: 1 of 2 Known
Value: $50,000

4.

1904 Liberty Double Eagle
Double Struck—ANACS MS-60 Prooflike

Double struck in the collar, this coin rotates several degrees counterclockwise between impressions. The obverse stars, Liberty's portrait, the date and the word LIBERTY inscribed on the coronet all exhibit a wide spread between the two strikes. The double-struck error is less dramatic on the reverse, but it is still visible upon careful examination.

Rarity: 2 Known
Value: $50,000

5.

1802/1 Capped Bust Right Half Eagle, BD-3, HBCC-3081, Miller-57, Rarity-4 (as a Die Pair)
Obverse Triple Struck—ANACS-Certified

This is an overdate Draped Bust $5 that has been struck three times on the obverse. It is an incredible major mint error on a 200 year old U.S. Gold coin.

The three separate strikes are clearly visible. Each strike shows a row of stars, the portrait, the Liberty Cap and the word Liberty above the portrait. This piece is one of only two known U.S. $5 Gold Coins that are struck three or more times.

Rarity: Unique
Value: $50,000

6.

Proof 1865 Gold Dollar
Reverse Triple Struck—PCGS Proof-64 Cameo

A unique multi-struck error on a proof 1865 Gold Dollar, this coin actually appears to have been struck upward of five times on the reverse. The multi-strike error occurred in the collar, and detail from each separate impression is discernible upon close examination with the aid of a loupe.

The 1865 is a very rare proof in the Gold Dollar series. Only 25 coins were originally struck, and many examples failed to survive this tumultuous final year of the Civil War. I believe that no more than 15-20 examples are known today, an estimate that includes this multi-struck error.

Rarity: Unique
Value: $50,000

7.

Great Britain, 1965 Penny, Spink-4157
Struck on a Gold Planchet—PCGS MS-62

Instead of being struck on a bronze planchet, this 1965 British Penny is struck on a gold planchet that weights 18.3 grams and is slightly larger than a United States Kennedy Half Dollar. I have neither seen nor heard rumor of a similar wrong planchet error on a British Penny.

Rarity: Unique
Value: $50,000

8.

1901/0-S Liberty Half Eagle, FS-301
Struck 10-15% Off-Center—PCGS AU-55

Although PCGS has certified this coin as being struck 10% off-center, I would describe it as being struck 15% off-center at 12 o'clock. The error has caused the planchet to expand to a greater size than that which is normal for a properly struck Liberty Half Eagle.

Free of all but the lightest friction, this Choice AU is even more desirable because the error occurred on an example of the 1901/0-S. This is a very bold overdate that is a scarce variety in its own right.

Rarity: 2 Known
Value: $50,000

9.

1803/2 Capped Bust Right Half Eagle, BD-3, HBCC-3081, Rarity-4 (as a Die Pair)
Misaligned Obverse Die—PCGS XF-45

The obverse die was misaligned in the press by 10% relative to the position of the reverse die, causing the obverse impression to be drawn toward the lower-right border of the coin. Although it is partially obscured, the date remains clearly visible. The reverse impression is properly centered, although the strike on that side of the coin is a bit soft along the lower-left border.

Major mint errors are rare even when they affect later-date U.S. gold coins beginning with the Liberty types introduced beginning in 1838. Early U.S. gold errors are even rarer and, indeed, I have never seen another misaligned die strike on an early Half Eagle of the Capped Bust Right, Capped Bust Left, Capped Head Left or Classic types.

Rarity: Unique
Value: $50,000

10.

1893-O Liberty Eagle
Broadstruck—PCGS AU-58

Another impressive example of a broadstruck error on a Liberty gold coin, this 1893-O Eagle was not seated in the collar when the dies came together during striking. The reeding around the edge is missing, and the diameter is greater than that which is normal for properly struck Liberty Eagles.

In addition to its status as a gold coin error, this 1893-O Eagle is of profound significance to specialized collectors because very few error coins of any kind are known from the New Orleans Mint.

Rarity: Unique
Value: $25,000

11.

1855 Three-Dollar Gold Piece
Broadstruck—PCGS AU-50

Some collectors might describe this coin as having been struck 5% off-center. In actuality, this is an uncentered broadstrike error on an 1855 Three-Dollar gold piece. Both sides retain most of the original mint luster, and the eye appeal is superior to what I would expect to see in a 19th century United States gold coin that grades "only" AU-50.

Three-Dollar gold pieces are scarce-to-rare pieces even as regular-issue type coins. Major mint errors on coins of this type are all but unknown. In fact, I believe that this error is one of only two broadstruck Three-Dollar gold pieces in existence. It is also the only such example dated 1855.

Rarity: 2 Known
Value: $20,000

12.

1897 Liberty Half Eagle
Struck 10% Off-Center—ANACS AU-55

A unique error when encountered on a Liberty Half Eagle that dates to 1897, this coin is struck 10% off-center at 6 o'clock. As with all off-center strikes, this piece is missing the reeding on the edge because it was struck out of the collar. Conservatively graded by ANACS, I believe that this coin is more accurately described as Mint State. There are no distracting abrasions or other blemishes evident to the naked eye.

Very few off-center errors are known in the U.S. gold series, and most examples are Indian Quarter Eagles that are struck only 3-5% off-center. An off-center error on a larger gold denomination is an extremely rare find, particularly when the strike is more than 5% off-center.

Rarity: 2 Known
Value: $15,000

13.

1912 Indian Quarter Eagle
Struck 10% Off-Center—PCGS AU-55

This gold coin is struck 10% off-center at 2 o'clock. The date is full, and the central design elements are boldly-to-sharply defined.

An important error, this Indian Quarter Eagle is one of very few U.S. gold coin errors of any denomination that is struck more than 5% off-center.

Rarity: 10-12 Known
Value: $15,000

14.

1855-C Liberty Half Eagle
Reverse Cud—NGC MS-61

The cud is located at the right-reverse rim outside the letters AMER in AMERICA.

Cuds are very rare errors on U.S. gold coins of any denomination or type, particularly when they are as large as the one on the reverse of the present coin. As a Mint State Charlotte Mint Half Eagle, this coin will appeal not only to error specialists, but also to collectors assembling high-grade sets of Southern gold coinage.

Rarity: 5 Known
Value: $12,500

15.

1857 Gold Dollar
Struck 5% Off-Center—PCGS AU-53

An early Philadelphia Mint issue in the Type III Gold Dollar series, this 1857 is struck a full 5% off-center at nearly 6 o'clock. The major design elements are not affected by the error, but some of the denticles along the lower-obverse and upper-reverse borders are either wholly or partially off the planchet.

Rarity: 5 Known
Value: $12,500

16.

1912 Indian Quarter Eagle
Struck 5% Off-Center—ANACS MS-63

The strike is a full 5% off-center at 3 o'clock, giving the appearance that this coin has an extra wide rim along the left border on both sides. The devices along the right borders are partially off the planchet.

Rarity: 10-12 Known
Value: $8,500

17.

Great Britain, 1876 ½ Sovereign, Spink-3860D
Reverse Full-Mirror Brockage—ANACS AU-58

The reverse displays a lovely first-strike brockage of the obverse design. As with all errors of this type, the brockage is incuse.

Brockage errors are rarely encountered on gold coins irrespective of country of origin, denomination or type.

Rarity: Unique
Value: $5,000

18.

Mexico, 1947 50 Pesos, Fr-172

Broadstruck—MS-62

Broadstruck out of the collar, the resulting coin looks as though it is struck 5% off-center at 5 o'clock.

I have encountered very few Mexican gold coin errors of any kind—a testament to the significance of this large 50 Peso piece.

Rarity: Unique
Value: $3,000

19.

Netherlands, 1928 Ducat, Fr-352

Struck 20% Off-Center—ANACS MS-66

The impression is off-center at 12 o'clock, which is one of the most desirable positions for error coins of this type.

I know of only two modern Ducats from the Netherlands that were struck off-center in error. The present example is Gem Mint State with full luster and beautiful surfaces.

Rarity: 2 Known
Value: $2,500

Price Guide for Gold Errors

Denomination	Partial Collar	Broadstruck	Clipped Planchet	3%-5% Off-Center	10%-15% Off-Center
$1 Gold Type 1	$2,500	$7,500	$2,000	$10,000	$25,000
$1 Gold Type 2	$5,000	$10,000	$10,000	$20,000	$35,000
$1 Gold Type 3	$2,000	$5,000	$1,500	$7,500	$15,000
$2½ Liberty	$2,000	$7,500	$2,500	$10,000	$20,000
$2½ Indian	$2,000	$7,500	$2,500	$7,500	$17,500
$3 Indian	$5,000	$15,000	$5,000	$15,000	$35,000
$5 Liberty	$3,000	$8,500	$3,000	$12,500	$30,000
$5 Indian	$4,000	$10,000	$3,000	$20,000	$40,000
$10 Liberty	$4,000	$12,500	$3,000	$25,000	$50,000
$10 Indian	$5,000	$15,000	$5,000	$30,000	$50,000
$20 Liberty	$7,500	$25,000	$7,500	$50,000	$150,000
$20 St. Gaudens	–	–	$5,000	–	–
$5 American Eagle	$1,000	$2,000	$750	$2,500	$3,500
$10 American Eagle	$1,250	$2,500	$1,000	$3,000	$3,500
$25 American Eagle	$1,500	$3,000	$1,500	$3,500	$5,000
$50 American Eagle	$2,000	$5,000	$2,000	$5,000	$10,000

Chapter 13

Hub and Die Trials

Hub and die trials are usually uniface (or struck on one side) impressions using either an obverse or reverse hub/die. These trials can be from either finished or unfinished designs. In either case, they are deliberate strikes to test the progress of a design and/or its suitability for regular-issue production.

Hub and die trials are often struck in metals other than those intended for regular-issue coinage. Softer metals such as tin and lead have often been used in the creation of hub and die trials, and there are some pieces known that were struck in cardboard or wax.

Traditionally, only pattern specialists pursued hub and die trials. Beginning in the late 1990s, however, I have seen increased demand for these pieces among error coin specialists who feel that these pieces would fit nicely into their collections due to their exotic appearance and the unusual circumstances under which they were produced.

1.

Undated Jefferson Nickel Reverse Die Trial, Judd-C1938-1

PCGS MS-62

Copper plated over a silver base metal. This important piece is a reverse die trial that features a portrait of Monticello that the Mint did not adopt for the regular-issue Jefferson Nickel design introduced in 1938. The proposed design is attributed to Anthony de Francisci, the artist that designed the Peace Dollar of 1921-1935.

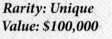

This coin is the only die trial known from the entire Jefferson Nickel series. It is the plate coin on page 318 of the 2005 book *United States Pattern Coins* by Dr. J. Hewitt Judd.

Rarity: Unique
Value: $100,000

2.

Undated (1838) Liberty Half Eagle Reverse Die Trial Splasher, Judd-A1838-6

PCGS MS-65

White metal. This die trial is a splasher and is struck on soft white metal using only the reverse die. The reverse is the Small Letters type used to strike regular-issue Liberty Half Eagles from 1839 through the early months of 1842. The die trial itself, however, was struck in 1838.

This piece is the plate coin on page 294 of the 2005 book *United States Pattern Coins*, Ninth Edition by Dr. J. Hewitt Judd.

Rarity: Unique
Value: $50,000

3.

1851 Three-Cent Silver Obverse & Reverse Die Trials, Judd-A185-1

As Struck

Cardboard. 0.35 millimeters thick, 85 millimeters x 50 millimeters. The card is glaze-surfaced and the impressions are clearly embossed with the devices and lettering fully defined. After the dies struck the cardboard, a bronze-gold ink was applied to show the high relief of the impressions to best effect.

This die trial is plated on page 296 of the 2005 book *United States Pattern Coins* by Dr. J. Hewitt Judd.

Rarity: Unique
Value: $40,000

4.

1910 Lincoln Cent Obverse Die Trial, Judd-Unlisted

PCGS AU-58

Bronze. This 1910 Lincoln Cent is a uniface die trial with sharp definition to all elements of the obverse design.

Despite the fact that the Lincoln Cent series is one of the most popular and widely collected in all of U.S. numismatics, this piece was unknown in general numismatic circles until the early years of the 21st century. It was the subject of a feature article in the September 22, 2003 issue of *Coin World*.

Rarity: Unique
Value: $40,000

5.

Undated (1860) Pattern Half Eagle Reverse Hub Trial, Judd-A1860-6

NGC MS-64 Brown

Copper. 31 millimeters. This remarkable piece is a reverse hub trial for the 1860 Judd-271 Pattern Half Eagle. Interestingly, only the legend UNITED STATES OF AMERICA and the denomination FIVE DOLLERS are present, both of which are incuse since this is a hub trial. The word DOLLERS is misspelled, and the letter V in FIVE is actually an inverted A. Neither of these seeming mistakes would have bothered Mint personnel in 1860 because their sole purpose in producing this hub trial was to test to layout of the inscriptions.

There are only 43 hub trials known for the entire United States pattern coin series. To place this figure into context we must remember that there are several thousand U.S. patterns known, as well as 272 splashers. This piece is the plate coin on page 300 of the 2005 book *United States Pattern Coins* by Dr. J. Hewitt Judd and page 410 of the 1994 book *United States Patterns and Related Issues* by Andrew W. Pollock III.

Ex: Robert Coulton Davis; F.C.C. Boyd; Rare Coins from the Abe Kosoff Estate (Bowers and Merena, 11/1985), lot 1166; Stack's sale of January 1989, lot 674. Dr. A. Roter.

Rarity: Unique
Value: $35,000

6.

1822 Capped Bust Half Dollar Double Struck Obverse Die Trial, Judd-A1822-A

NGC MS-64 Brown

Copper. A double struck uniface die trial, there are two complete impressions of Liberty's portrait as well as the stars, date and denticles. This piece was struck outside the Mint from a discarded die that is not listed in the 2005 book *United States Early Half Dollar Die Varieties: 1794-1836* by Donald L. Parsley (based on earlier editions of the same title by Al C. Overton).

The present example is the plate coin on page 292 of the 2005 book *United States Pattern Coins* by Dr. J. Hewitt Judd.

Rarity: 5 Known
Value: $25,000

7.

1865 Anthony C. Paquet Andrew Johnson/George Washington Medal Uniface Die Trial Splasher Pair

As Struck

White Metal. Struck in high relief, these unique splashers have been remarkably well preserved considering that they were prepared during the chaotic final year of the U.S. Civil War.

These splashers were created by Assistant Engraver Anthony C. Paquet. The obverse depicts a right-facing bust of President Andrew Johnson. The reverse depicts an Indian peace motif with a small bust of President George Washington.

Rarity: Unique
Value: $25,000

8.

Undated (1857) Pattern Half Dollar Reverse Die Trial, Judd-A1857-A

NGC MS-63

White metal. The reverse design used to create this die trial is credited to Assistant Engraver Anthony C. Paquet, who prepared many of the pattern coins struck in the U.S. Mint during the late 1850s. An unfinished design, this die was never used to strike any pattern or regular-issue coinage for the United States.

This piece is plated on page 296 of the 2005 book *United States Pattern Coins* by Dr. J. Hewitt Judd and also on page 404 of the 1994 book *United States Patterns and Related Issues* by Andrew W. Pollock III.

Ex: Stephen K. Nagy; 1958 ANA Sale; Rare Coins from the Abe Kosoff Estate (Bowers and Merena, 11/1985), lot 1147; Jascha Heifetz Collection Sale (Superior, 10/1989), lot 3398.

Rarity: Unique
Value: $10,000

9.

Undated (1877) Pattern Half Union Reverse Hub Trial, Judd-A1877-11

NGC-Certified

Lead. This is the unique reverse hub trial of the famous pattern 1877 $50 Half Union. It is plated on page 306 of the 2005 edition of the book *United States Pattern Coins* by Dr. J. Hewitt Judd. Only the eagle, scroll, arrows and laurel branches in the reverse design are present.

Ex: Stephen K. Nagy; 1958 ANA Sale; Kagin's Sale of November 1964); Bowers and Ruddy Galleries (5/1973); 1993 Baltimore ANA Sale (Heritage, 7/1993), lot 5883.

Rarity: Unique
Value: $10,000

10.

Pattern 1867 Five-Cent Piece Obverse Hub Trial, Judd-A1867-9

NGC MS-63 Brown

Copper. The device punches used to prepare this hub trial were also intended for use in the production of working dies, hence the incuse and inverted nature of the devices on this piece.

This hub trial is plated on page 302 of the 2005 book *United States Pattern Coins* by Dr. J. Hewitt Judd.

Rarity: Unique
Value: $10,000

11.

Pattern 1867 Five-Cent Piece Obverse & Reverse Hub Trial, Judd-A1867-15

NGC MS-64 Brown

Copper. This unique obverse and reverse hub trial shows the incomplete design of Liberty's portrait that the Mint later used to strike patterns in nickel and copper with a plain edge (Judd-566/Pollock-627 and Judd-567/Pollock-628).

This obverse and reverse hub trial gives us a glimpse into Longacre's creative process by illustrating a design that he made, and then personally changed before he arrived at his final product. It is the plate coin on page 302 of the 2005 book *United States Pattern Coins* by. Dr. J. Hewitt Judd and also on page 413 of the 1994 book *United States Patterns and Related Issues* by Andrew W, Pollock III.

Ex: Major Lenox R. Lohr; Robert Batchelder; R.B. White; Kissel & Victoria Collections (Bowers and Merena, 9/1989), lot 2583.

Rarity: Unique
Value: $10,000

12.

Switzerland, 1855 Pattern 5 Francs Obverse & Reverse Die Trial Klippe

MS-63 Prooflike

Silver. This piece is double struck with mirror-finish surfaces and beautiful sea-green toning. All Swiss patterns are rare, and this klippe is of even greater desirability due to the exceptional eye appeal that it possesses.

Rarity: 5 Known
Value: $3,500

Price Guide for Hub and Die Trials

Prices fluctuate due to the date, grade, eye appeal and how dramatic the striking error is. Rarity is also a factor. The price is sometimes based on the rarity and grade of the type of coin as well as how rare the error is. There is no price guide for this chapter because of the extreme rarity and low number of errors available.

An indent error occurs when two planchets are inadvertently fed into the same collar, with one planchet partially overlapping the other. When the hammer die strikes this combination, the upper planchet is forced into the lower planchet and creates a depression in the metal that is shaped like the upper planchet.

A very rare type of indent error is one that involves planchets intended for two different denominations.

I.

1971-D Kennedy Half Dollar

Reverse Indent from a Cent Planchet—ANACS MS-62

The indent is just above center on the reverse, and it obscures much of the eagle as well as part of the legend UNITED STATES OF AMERICA. The fact that the indent is so well centered on the reverse, however, confirms this as one of the most appealing errors of this type that I ever handled.

United States coins that are fully indented by smaller blank planchets are very rare errors.

Rarity: 5 Known
Value: $5,000

2.

1971-D Eisenhower Dollar
Reverse Indent from a Cent Planchet—PCGS MS-63

The indent covers the left portion of the reverse, obscuring most of the eagle, more than half of the Latin motto E PLURIBUS UNUM and much of the word UNITED in the legend UNIT-ED STATES OF AMERICA.

Like the Kennedy Half Dollar pictured on the previous page, this Eisenhower Dollar is a particularly desirable indent error because the outline of the entire Cent planchet is present on the struck coin.

Rarity: 3 Known
Value: $5,000

3.

Undated Indian Cent
Obverse 40% Indent from a Cent Planchet—NGC MS-66

The indent is positioned over the lower reverse, where it obscures the entire date area as well as the lower portion of Liberty's portrait. The appearance of the final product is very dramatic.

Although this is not a particularly rare error for a coin of this type, very few indented Indian Cents are encountered in Gem Mint State. This piece is easily among the finest known.

Rarity: 20-50 Known
Value: $1,500

4.

Undated Liberty Nickel
Obverse 40% Indent from a Nickel Planchet—PCGS AU-55

This coin has a 40% indent on the obverse from a blank planchet that was also supposed to be struck into a Liberty Nickel. The indent obliterated the lower left quadrant of the obverse design, including most of the date. The final digit—an 8—is readily evident, however, but it is not possible to determine whether this Liberty Nickel error was struck in 1888, 1898 or 1908. Partial definition to the obverse further enhances already strong eye appeal.

Rarity: 10 Known
Value: $1,000

Price Guide for Indents

Denomination	10% - 25% XF	30% - 50% XF	10% - 25% Unc	30% - 50% Unc
Large Cent	$300	$600	$750	$2,000
Indian Cent	$250	$500	$400	$750
Lincoln Cent 1943 Steel	$100	$300	$175	$500
Lincoln Cent Wheat Ears	$30	$75	$75	$125
3 Cent Nickel	$500	$1,250	$1,500	$3,000
Shield Nickel	$500	$1,500	$2,000	$3,000
Liberty Nickel	$400	$1,000	$750	$1,500
Buffalo Nickel	$300	$1,000	$600	$2,000
Jefferson Nickel War Time	$200	$400	$400	$750
Jefferson Nickel	$10	$25	$15	$30
Barber Dime	$1,000	$2,000	$1,500	$3,000
Mercury Dime	$300	$750	$500	$1,500
Roosevelt Dime Silver	$30	$60	$50	$100
Roosevelt Dime Clad	$10	$20	$15	$30
Washington Quarter Silver	$100	$200	$150	$300
Washington Quarter Clad	$25	$50	$35	$100
State Quarter	N/A	N/A	$200	$350
Kennedy Half Clad	$150	$300	$200	$400
Eisenhower Dollar	$350	$1,000	$500	$1,500
Susan B Anthony Dollar	N/A	N/A	$250	$500
Sacagawea Dollar	N/A	N/A	$400	$750

Chapter 15

Martha Washington Test Pieces

*T*here is one set of a Dime, Quarter and Half struck by Martha Washington dies that are permanently housed in the Smithsonian Institute, embedded in blocks of lucite. According to United States Pattern and Related Issues, *by Andrew W. Pollock III, "the only trial pieces purported to have survived metallurgical testing in 1965 were the Dime, Quarter Dollar, and Half Dollar equivalent strikes in copper-nickel clad over copper."*

My discovery of the Martha Washington Test Piece on a copper-zinc Cent planchet struck 10% off-center with a uniface reverse was a front page Coin World article on August 7th, 2000. In a response to the Martha Washington Test Piece that I discovered, the Mint announced that "the dies are available to the Mint's metal and blank vendors for testing."

1.

"1759" Martha Washington Experimental Dollar-Size Medal

Judd-2184, Experimental Edge, NGC MS-64 Prooflike

Copper-nickel clad. 8.0 grams. This Martha Washington test piece is struck on a copper-nickel clad Susan B. Anthony Dollar planchet with an experimental edge. The edge is intermittently reeded.

Rarity: Unique
Value: $50,000

2.

"1759" Martha Washington Experimental Dollar-Size Medal

Judd-Unlisted, Experimental Edge, NGC MS-64

Magnesium brass-coated, copper-clad metal. 8.0 grams. This piece was struck in 1999 in the alloy that the Mint would adopt for regular-issue Sacagawea Dollar production in 2000. It has an experimental edge that features intermittent reeding.

Rarity: Unique
Value: $35,000

3.

"1759" Martha Washington Experimental Quarter-Size Medal

Judd-2116, NGC MS-65

Cupronickel-copper. 5.7 grams. This Martha Washington test piece dates to 1965 and is one of only four examples of Judd-2116 in private hands. It is the plate coin for the type on page 294 of the 2005 book *United States Pattern Coins* by Dr. J. Hewitt Judd.

Rarity: 4 Known
Value: $20,000

4.

"1759" Martha Washington Experimental Dollar-Size Medal

Judd-2185, NGC MS-65

Magnesium brass-coated, copper-clad metal. 8.0 grams. This Martha Washington test piece was struck in 1999 as part of the Mint's search for a suitable alloy for the Sacagawea Dollar introduced in 2000.

Rarity: 5 Known
Value: $20,000

5.

"1759" Martha Washington Experimental Half Dollar-Size Medal

Judd-2132, NGC MS-63

Cupronickel-copper. 11.23 grams. Dating to 1965, this piece was produced as part of the Mint's search for a suitable replacement for the 90% silver, 10% copper alloy that had been used to strike Half Dollars since the 1836.

Rarity: 3 Known
Value: $12,500

6.

"1759" Martha Washington Experimental Cent-Size Medal

Judd-2180, NGC MS-66 Red and Brown

Copper-zinc alloy. 2.5 grams. This Martha Washington piece was almost certainly used in the tests for a new Cent alloy that the Mint conducted in 1982. The composition is similar to that adopted for regular-issue Cent production partway through 1982, but the alloy is 97.5% zinc, 2.5% copper as opposed to 99.2% zinc, 0.8% copper with a pure plating of copper.

Rarity: 3 Known
Value: $7,500

7.

"1759" Martha Washington Experimental Five-Cent Piece-Size Medal

Judd-2182, NGC MS-63

Nickel. 5.0 grams. This Martha Washington test piece dates to 1985 and is struck on a Five-Cent-size planchet.

Rarity: 5 Known
Value: $7,500

8.

Undated ("1759") Experimental Cent Obverse Die Trial

Judd-A1982-1, NGC-Certified

Copper-Nickel. 2.5 grams. A uniface die trial, the obverse impression is 10% off center at 5 o'clock.

This piece was struck using the Martha Washington/Mount Vernon experimental design with the fantasy date 1759. It was produced in 1982, possibly by one of the private firms engaged in finding a suitable replacement for the bronze alloy that the Mint used to strike Cents from late 1864 through early 1982. This die trial is plated on page 312 of the 2005 book *United States Pattern Coins* by Dr. J. Hewitt Judd.

My discovery of this coin was reported in a front page article in the August 7, 2000 issue of *Coin World* magazine. After I made this discovery, the Mint announced that it had made the Martha Washington experimental dies available to private vendors for testing purposes. It is likely that this obverse die trial for the 1982 Experimental Cent is attributed to a private vendor and not the U.S. Mint.

Ex: California Sale (Ira & Larry Goldberg, 10/2000), lot 1972; Rarities Sale (Bowers and Merena, 1/2003) lot 996.

Rarity: Unique
Value: $5,000

Price Guide for Martha Washington Test Pieces

Denomination	UNC	Choice	GEM
Martha Cent	$5,000	$6,000	$7,500
Martha Nickel	$4,000	$6,000	$7,500
Martha Dime	$20,000	$30,000	$50,000
Martha Quarter	$15,000	$20,000	$30,000
Martha Half Dollar	$10,000	$12,500	$15,000
Martha Dollar (Susan B Anthony Planchet)	--	--	$50,000
Martha Dollar (Sacagawea Planchet)	$10,000	$15,000	$20,000

Chapter 16

Mated Pairs

M ated pairs involve two individual coins with different errors that were struck together at the same time. Mated pair error combinations can be found in most error types and come in many shapes and sizes. Mated pairs can be overlapped when one of the coins is struck off-center on top of another coin. Another type involves a brockage where a struck coin is perfectly centered on a blank and restruck. Some mated pairs involve a die cap where the cap and brockage coin are discovered together, but this is a scarce find.

The rarest mated pair type involves two die caps (obverse and reverse) where both dies are capped at the same time and both die caps are mated. This last type is extremely rare and there are only a few known examples of mated pairs involving an obverse die cap and reverse die cap. There are several of these mated pairs known on Kennedy Halves including two that are dated 1976, which is the Bicentennial year.

Mated pairs can also involve an off-metal where a smaller blank planchet or smaller struck coin was struck on top of a larger coin. This type is extremely rare. The most spectacular pair known is a double struck Franklin Half that was mated to a Lincoln Cent. The Lincoln Cent blank was on top of the obverse of the struck Franklin Half. This unique pair was then struck together.

1.

1963 Franklin Half Dollar

Mated Pair of Wrong Planchet and Indent Errors—PCGS MS-62 and MS-66

This exciting error was created when a Cent planchet came to rest over the lower half of a Half Dollar planchet in a press that the Mint was using to strike Franklin Half Dollars. The resulting impression from the dies created an off-metal error out of the Cent planchet and a dramatic indent out of the Half Dollar planchet. The Cent fit snugly into the indent.

This mated pair was once part of an old-time collection, and it has since become widely known as one of the most important mated pair error in all of U.S. numismatics.

Rarity: Unique
Value: $50,000

2.

1986 Silver Eagle

Mated Pair of a Reverse Strikethrough and a Sanding Disk—PCGS MS-66

A three-millimeter sanding disk adhered to the reverse die and was struck into the reverse of a planchet that was subsequently fed into the press. The sanding disk is thin enough that the reverse design is still visible on the coin, although it has a noticeable "fuzzy" appearance due to the strike through. Both pieces were released from the Mint together and the pair has been intact ever since.

This mated pair is one of the most unusual errors struck in the modern U.S. Mint.

Rarity: 2 Known
Value: $12,500

3.

1965 Kennedy Half Dollar

Mated Pair of a Double-Struck, Broadstruck and Indent Errors—As Struck

The first coin in this mated pair features a double-struck reverse with a 20% indent over the upper portion of the obverse. The second coin is a broadstruck indent. Both pieces fit snugly together at the indent.

Rarity: Unique
Value: $7,500

4.

1979 Kennedy Half Dollar
Mated Pair of a Die Cap, Brockage and Counter-brockage Errors—ANACS AU-55 and MS-62

Very similar to the mated pair of 1979 Kennedy Half Dollars on the next page, the first coin in this pair is a double-struck fli-pover obverse with a counterbrockage reverse. The second coin is double struck with an obverse brockage.

There are only two mated pair errors known for the 1979 Kennedy Half Dollar, both of which are presented in this book.

Rarity: 2 Known
Value: $7,500

5.

1976-D Bicentennial Kennedy Half Dollar
Mated Pair of Obverse and Reverse Die Caps—ANACS MS-65 and MS-60

Both the obverse and reverse dies were capped when this extraordinary mated pair was struck. The reverse of the obverse die cap is a brockage that created a counterbrockage on the obverse of the reverse die cap. Both the brockage and the counterbrockage are relatively clear, which suggests that both die caps left the press immediately after formation of this mated pair.

Only two Kennedy Half Dollar mated pair errors are known in which both coins in the pair are die caps.

Rarity: 2 Known
Value: $7,500

6.

1981 Lincoln Cent
Mated Pair of Obverse and Reverse Die Caps—MS-62 Brown

This error pair features a double-struck obverse die cap mated to a multi-struck reverse die cap. The obverse of the reverse die cap is a brockage struck from the reverse of the other coin.

Most Lincoln Cent die caps are dated 1999 and, as such, they are struck on copper-plated zinc planchets. This mated pair, however, was struck in 1981 on bronze planchets.

Rarity: 10 Known
Value: $1,000

7.

Mexico, Undated 5 Pesos, KM-482
Mated Pair of Wrong Planchet, Indent and Brockage Errors—ANACS MS-64

The KM-482 attribution dates this error to the 1970s. Only the first two digits in the date are discernible, however, and then again only on the second example. The first coin is struck on a 20 Centavos planchet in error. It then indented and caused a partial brockage on the obverse of another 5 Pesos coin. This is an extraordinary set.

Rarity: Unique
Value: $750

Price Guide for Mated Pairs

Denomination	Overlapping	Full Brockage	Die Cap	2 Die Caps
Lincoln Cent Wheat Ears	$3,500	$4,500	$7,500	–
Lincoln Cent Memorial	$500	$750	$750	$1,250
Liberty Nickel	–	$20,000	–	–
Jefferson Nickel (pre-War Time)	–	–	–	$15,000
Jefferson Nickel	$1,000	$1,250	$1,500	$2,500
Barber Dime	–	–	–	$50,000
Roosevelt Dime Silver	$3,500	$4,000	$4,000	–
Roosevelt Dime Clad	$1,000	$1,250	$2,500	$3,000
Washington Quarter Silver	$4,000	–	–	–
Washington Quarter Clad	$1,500	$2,500	$5,000	$7,500
State Quarter	$3,000	$5,000	$10,000	–
Kennedy Half Silver	$7,500	$7,500	$7,500	$12,500
Kennedy Half Clad	$5,000	$6,000	$6,000	$8,500
Kennedy Half Bicentennial	$6,000	$7,500	$7,500	$10,000
Eisenhower Dollar	$20,000	–	–	–
Susan B Anthony Dollar	$7,500	$10,000	–	–
Sacagawea Dollar	–	–	–	–

Chapter 17

Mules

A mule is a coin struck with a mismatched combination of dies. In some countries, the Mints use dies of identical dimensions to strike coins of different denominations and/or for other countries. In these instances, mules have been reported for many years and are not really rare items. An example is a mule between a Bahamas 5 Cents obverse and a New Zealand 2 Cents reverse. Thousands of these errors were struck, and individual examples are worth only $50.

Mules involving United States coins, however, are exceedingly rare and carry price tags in the thousands of dollars. One of the most famous U.S. Mint mules is the Statehood Quarter obverse/Sacagawea Dollar reverse discovered in early 2000.

1.

1999 Lincoln Cent Obverse Muled with a Roosevelt Dime Reverse

PCGS MS-65

This unique 1999 Lincoln Cent was struck with a reverse die intended for a Roosevelt Dime. The reverse detail is very sharp, while that on the reverse is weak along the left border. This coin is struck on a copper-plated zinc planchet, as is normal for Lincoln Cents produced beginning in 1982.

Rarity: Unique
Value: $125,000

2.

1995 Roosevelt Dime Reverse Muled with a Lincoln Cent Obverse

PCGS MS-66

The planchet is copper-nickel as intended for a Roosevelt Dime and, indeed, the reverse was struck from a Roosevelt Dime die. The obverse, however, was struck from the obverse die of a 1995 Lincoln Cent.

Rarity: Unique
Value: $125,000

3.

1993-D Lincoln Cent Obverse Muled with a Roosevelt Dime Reverse

PCGS MS-64

This mule is struck on a copper-plated zinc planchet as intended for a properly produced Lincoln Cent.

Rarity: Unique
Value: $125,000

4.

Great Britain, Dual-Dated 1829/1823 ½ Sovereign Mule

PCGS Proof-63 Cameo

The obverse die is the type used to strike ½ Sovereigns dated 1826-1828, and it is attributed as Fr-380. Interestingly, however, no regular-issue 1829 Half Sovereigns were struck either in proof or business strike formats. The reverse is a pattern die with a crowned shield in the center and the inscription ANNO 1823 around the border. A rose, shamrock and thistle are below the shield.

There are only two examples of this fascinating mule known to exist, and the other coin is impounded in the Royal Mint Collection. The piece pictured here, therefore, is the only one available for private ownership. No other gold mules are known regardless of denomination or country of origin. If this error were a product of the U.S. Mint, it would easily command a price of $500,000+ in the numismatic market of the early 21st century.

Rarity: 2 Known
Value: $50,000

Price Guide for Mules

Prices fluctuate due to the date, grade, eye appeal and how dramatic the striking error is. Rarity is also a factor. The price is sometimes based on the rarity and grade of the type of coin as well as how rare the error is. There is no price guide for this chapter because of the extreme rarity and low number of errors available.

Chapter 18

Off-Center Strikes

Off-center coins are one of the most common and widely recognized errors in the numismatic market. This type of error is created when a planchet is improperly fed into the press and is not seated perfectly in the collar. When the dies strike the planchet, only that part of the planchet that overlays the collar will receive a portion of the coin's design.

1.

1904 Liberty Double Eagle
Struck 15% Off-Center—PCGS-Certified

This incredible Liberty Double Eagle is the farthest off-center error known for a United States gold coin. It is struck approximately 15% off-center at 5 o'clock. The coin grades Choice Mint State.

Ex: Fred Weinberg.

Rarity: Unique
Value: $250,000

2.

1880-S Morgan Silver Dollar
Struck 40% Off-Center—PCGS MS-63

This coin was discovered in a sealed bag of 1880 Morgan Dollars from the San Francisco Mint. It is one of the finest off-center errors known from the 1878-1921 Morgan Dollar series. This 1880-S is struck 40% off-center at 12 o'clock. The clock position is ideal for an error of this type since it allows full appreciation of the date. Many consider this off-center Morgan to be the finest known example for the series.

Rarity: 20-50 Known
Value: $125,000

3.

1921-S Morgan Silver Dollar
Struck 45% Off-Center—NGC MS-63

The strike is off-center at 7 o'clock which means that, while the S mint-mark on the reverse is clearly evident, the date is off the planchet on the obverse. Fortunately, the Mint adopted a modified design for the Morgan Dollar in 1921, so this error had to be struck during the final year of this long-lived and extremely popular series.

Morgan Dollars that are slightly off-center (or even as much as 10-20% off-center if they are in circulated condition) are only scarce when viewed in the wider context of the U.S. error coin market. Any example that is struck more than 20% off-center is rare, however, particularly if it is also Mint State. The present example is one of only two Morgan Dollars errors known that are struck this far off center.

Rarity: 20-50 Known
Value: $60,000

4.

Undated Large Eagle Draped Bust Silver Dollar
Struck 15% Off-Center—PCGS VF-35

A well-known and highly regarded rarity in the error coin community, this piece is the farthest off-center Draped Bust Dollar error known. The impression is off-center at 4 o'clock. Both sides are attractively toned, and the coin has the appearance of an XF grade.

Rarity: Unique
Value: $35,000

5.

1918-S Standing Liberty Quarter
Struck 13% Off-Center—PCGS MS-63 Full Head

This early date, San Francisco Mint Standing Liberty Quarter is struck 13% off-center at 12-1 o'clock. Since it was struck out of the collar, there is also no reeding on the edge.

Major errors of all kinds are seldom encountered on Standing Liberty Quarters. This particular example is pictured on page 79 of J.H. Cline's book *Standing Liberty Quarters*, Zyrus Press, 2007, where the author describes it as, "A very beautiful piece."

Rarity: 5 Known
Value: $30,000

6.

1944 Walking Liberty Half Dollar
Struck 40% Off-Center—ANACS VF-20

This coin is struck farther off-center than any other Walking Liberty Half Dollar known. The impression is off-center at 12 o'clock. The date is discernible, but the mintmark position is off the planchet on the reverse. As such, it is not possible to determine whether this coin was struck in the Philadelphia, Denver or San Francisco Mint. The considerable wear that both sides exhibit suggests that a previous owner carried this coin as a pocket piece for many years. It is certainly a dramatic error, and it could still be used as an interesting conversation piece.

Off-center Walking Liberty Half Dollars are extremely rare, and most examples that are encountered in today's market are only struck 5-10% off-center.

Rarity: 5 Known
Value: $15,000

7.

Undated New Orleans Mint Morgan Silver Dollar

Struck 25% Off-Center—PCGS XF-45

Although upward of 50 off-center errors are known from the Morgan Dollar series, most examples are only slightly off-center. This impressive piece, on the other hand, is a full 25% off-center at 5 o'clock. The O mintmark on the reverse is readily evident, and all devices that made it onto the planchet are actually quite bold.

Rarity: 20-50 Known
Value: $15,000

8.

1857 Flying Eagle Cent

Struck 25% Off-Center—NGC AU-55

The strike is off-center at 3 o'clock, with the result that all four digits in the date are still readily evident. Additionally, most of the eagle is present on the obverse, and only half of the right-reverse wreath is off the planchet on the reverse.

Only a few off-center errors in the Flying Eagle Cent series are known, and most are struck only 5-10% off-center.

Rarity: 10 Known
Value: $15,000

9.

Undated Coronet Large Cent

Struck 35% Off-Center—NGC MS-64 Brown

Nearly in the Gem category, this sharp-looking Coronet Cent is off-center at 7 o'clock.

Off-center large Cents are relatively plentiful as far as U.S. Mint errors are concerned. On the other hand, most such errors are only 5-20% off-center, and they are typically encountered well worn. This high-grade example, therefore, is an extremely important coin both due to the nature of the error and the level of preservation.

Rarity: 20-50 Known
Value: $15,000

10.

1795 Flowing Hair Silver Dollar, Three Leaves, B-7, BB-18, Rarity-4 (as a Die Pair)

Struck 5% Off-Center—NGC VF-30

An impressive error that has been well-documented for many years, this early Dollar is struck 5% off-center at 10 o'clock. It is the only off-center error from the two-year Flowing Hair Dollar series of 1794-1795.

Rarity: Unique
Value: $10,000

11.

1922-S Peace Dollar
Struck 5% Off-Center—PCGS MS-62

Struck 5% off-center at 1 o'clock, this coin is also broadstruck.

This is a very rare type as an off-center error. In fact, off-center Peace Dollars are hundreds of times rarer than similar errors from the Morgan Dollar series.

Rarity: 2-3 Known
Value: $10,000

12.

1879-S Morgan Silver Dollar
Struck 15% Off-Center—PCGS MS-61 Prooflike

This second-year Morgan Dollar from the San Francisco Mint is struck 15% off-center. Although the error is in the 6 o'clock position, a partial date is still present on the obverse.

Most off-center Morgan Dollar errors fall within the VF-AU grade range—a fact that speaks volumes about the significance of this Mint State example.

Rarity: 20-50 Known
Value: $8,500

13.

1861 Seated Quarter
Struck 15% Off-Center—PCGS AU-58

The strike is off-center at 5 o'clock with the date still fully evident on the obverse. Overall sharply struck, this coin is just the lightest rub away from a Mint State grade.

This is a very rare error for a Seated Quarter, particularly a No Motto example struck prior to 1866.

Rarity: 5-10 Known
Value: $7,500

14.

1903 Barber Half Dollar
Struck 20% Off-Center—PCGS XF-45

Struck off-center at 9 o'clock, this lightly worn example retains a full date and plenty of bold definition to Liberty's portrait and the reverse eagle.

Off-center errors in the Barber Half Dollar series are much rarer than they are in the Morgan Dollar series. This 1903 is the only Barber Half Dollar known that is struck more than 10% off-center.

Rarity: 10 Known
Value: $7,500

15.

1900-O Barber Half Dollar
Struck 10% Off-Center—PCGS AU-50

This New Orleans Mint Barber Half Dollar is struck a full 10% off-center at 2 o'clock. Both sides exhibit original toning over surfaces that are still predominantly lustrous.

Rarity: 10 Known
Value: $7,500

16.

1911 Indian Quarter Eagle
Struck 5% Off-Center—ANACS MS-64

The strike is off-center at nearly the 6 o'clock position. The date is only partially visible, but all four digits are clearly discernible.

This is the "type coin" among off-center U.S. gold errors. Since there are only 10-12 Indian Quarter Eagles known that have been struck off-center, however, this 1911 is still an extremely rare coin when viewed in the wider context of the numismatic market.

Rarity: 10-12 Known
Value: $6,000

17.

1859 Indian Cent
Struck 15% Off-Center—NGC MS-64

Off-center at the 7 o'clock position, this coin still displays a full date on the obverse. Additionally, none of the reverse devices are affected by the error.

Rarity: 10 Known
Value: $6,000

18.

1976 Bicentennial Eisenhower Dollar
Struck 50% Off-Center, Obverse Brockage—MS-63

A remarkable error, this coin is struck 50% off-center with an obverse brockage from another off-center Bicentennial Eisenhower Dollar.

This is a rare and visually impressive double error from this one-year type in the Dollar series.

Rarity: 10 Known
Value: $6,000

19.

1873 Arrows Seated Dime
Struck 12% Off-Center—PCGS AU-55

Struck 12% off-center at 1 o'clock, this Seated Dime displays a full date and overall sharp definition to the devices.

Very few Seated Dime errors of all kinds are known to exist, and the present example is even more important because it was struck on an example of the short-lived Arrows, Legend Obverse type of 1873-1874.

Rarity: 2 Known
Value: $5,000

20.

1999-P Susan B. Anthony Dollar
Struck 60% Off-Center on a Quarter Planchet—PCGS MS-65

An impressive double error, this Anthony Dollar is struck 60% off-center at 1 o'clock on a copper-nickel clad Quarter planchet. Both the date and the P mintmark are readily evident at the upper-right obverse.

Multiple errors in the Anthony Dollar series are rare and seldom encountered in numismatic circles.

Rarity: 3 Known
Value: $3,000

Price Guide for Off-Center Strikes

Denomination	10% - 15% XF/AU	25% - 60% XF/AU	10% - 15% Unc	25% - 60% Unc
Large Cent	$400	$2,500	$1,000	$10,000
Flying Eagle Cent (1857–1858)	$2,500	$10,000	$5,000	$20,000
Indian Cent	$100	$400	$200	$600
Lincoln Cent 1930 and Earlier	$75	$300	$150	$750
Lincoln Cent 1943 Steel	$40	$250	$100	$500
Proof Lincoln Cent	N/A	N/A	$1,500	$3,000
3 Cent Nickel	$300	$1,500	$600	$3,500
3 Cent Silver	$1,000	$5,000	$2,000	$7,500
Shield Nickel	$750	$2,500	$1,000	$7,500
Liberty Nickel	$250	$1,000	$500	$2,500
Buffalo Nickel	$250	$750	$400	$1,500
Jefferson Nickel War Time	$100	$500	$200	$1,000
Proof Jefferson Nickel	N/A	N/A	$2,000	$5,000
Seated Half Dime Legend	$3,000	$7,500	$5,000	$15,000
Seated Dime Legend	$2,000	$7,000	$3,500	$10,000
Barber Dime	$300	$1,500	$500	$2,500
Mercury Dime	$100	$750	$150	$1,250
Proof Clad Dime	N/A	N/A	$2,500	$5,000
Barber Quarter	$1,500	$5,000	$2,500	$10,000
Standing Liberty Quarter	$5,000	$20,000	$20,000	$40,000
Washington Quarter Silver	$50	$100	$75	$150
State Quarter	N/A	N/A	$75	$300
Proof Clad Quarter	N/A	N/A	$3,000	$7,500
Barber Half	$4,000	$10,000	$6,000	$20,000
Walking Liberty Half	$4,000	$12,500	$7,500	$20,000
Franklin Half	$2,500	$4,000	$3,500	$7,500
Kennedy Half Silver	$100	$500	$250	$1,000
Kennedy Half Clad	$60	$250	$100	$400
Proof Clad Half	N/A	N/A	$4,000	$7,500
Morgan Dollar	$3,000	$15,000	$10,000	$50,000
Peace Dollar	$20,000	$75,000	$75,000	$125,000
Eisenhower Dollar	$125	$1,250	$150	$2,000
Susan B Anthony Dollar	N/A	N/A	$100	$500
Sacagawea Dollar	N/A	N/A	$1,000	$3,500
Presidential Dollar	Unknown	Unknown	Unknown	Unknown

Chapter 19
Overstrikes

Overstrikes are coins that have been struck over a struck coin. Generally speaking, there are two major types of overstrikes. The first type would be a double denomination (a Lincoln Cent struck over a struck Dime). Although these are overstrikes, they are referred to as double denominations and are known on many denominations of coins from many countries.

The other main type of overstrike is a coin which is struck (either deliberately or as a mint error) on a previously struck coin from a different era and country. In ancient times, it was not uncommon to strike coins over previously struck coins with portraits of earlier Kings. In Colonial times, coins circulating were sometimes struck using other coins that were in circulation, regardless of whether they were from the country striking the coin or from a different country.

A rare example of an overstrike is a 1915 Panama Half Commem which was struck in Proof over a cut down St. Gaudens $20 gold piece. The example on this page is a rare overstrike from Panama.

1.

Paraguay, Four-Piece Pattern Set

Overstruck on Gold Coins from Chile and Argentina—NGC MS-66 and MS-65

This is a unique four-piece set 19th century Paraguay pattern coins overstruck on previously struck gold coins from Chile and Argentina. Certified by NGC, this spectacular discovery set was published as a cover story in the Fall 2005 edition (Issue 11) of *Mint Error News Magazine*.

What is particularly fascinating about this set is that the dies for each of the four patterns were unfinished and include only the first two digits of the date. Additionally, several of the gold coins from Chile and Argentina that were used as planchets for the Paraguay pattern dies are rare types or issues. All were in high levels of preservation, which indicates that they were hand selected for this purpose. Based on this evidence, I believe that these four coins are a presentation set that was struck in an official government mint and has since been preserved with the utmost care on the part of its various owners.

Rarity: Unique
Value: $100,000

First Coin in Set:

Paraguay, Pattern 18XX Peso—Overstruck on a Chile, 1849 8 Escudos, Fr-41

NGC MS-66

Due to its large size, high level of preservation and the amount of detail that is discernible from both sets of designs, this is the most visually impressive piece in this set. A lovely Gem.

Second Coin in Set:

Paraguay, Pattern 18XX 50 Centavos—Overstruck on a Chile, 1853 10 Pesos, Fr-45

NGC MS-66

Once again, considerable definition from the undertype is still readily evident on both sides of this dramatic piece. Since the Chile 10 Pesos coin was smaller than the dies for the Paraguay pattern 50 Centavos, most of the remaining design elements from the former type are discernible at the borders.

Third Coin in Set:

Paraguay, Pattern 18XX 50 Centavos— Overstruck on a Chile, 1859 10 Pesos, Fr-45

NGC MS-65

This piece is struck from the same pattern 50 Centavos dies as those used to create the other pattern 50 Centavos overstrike in this set. Considerable portions of the Chile 10 Pesos design remain on both sides.

Fourth Coin in Set:

Paraguay, Pattern 18XX 20 Centavos— Overstruck on an Argentina, 1887 5 Pesos, Fr-14

NGC MS-65

Unlike the other three coins in this set, this pattern 20 Centavos is overstruck on a gold piece from Argentina. It is an attractive Gem with plenty of detail to the undertype still readily evident.

2.

Philippines, Undated Piso, KM-203
Overstruck on an Undated Washington Quarter—PCGS MS-64

The Philippine Piso dies were impressed into a struck Washington Quarter approximately 30% off-center at 2 o'clock. Additionally, the Quarter is rotated approximately 15 degrees counterclockwise in relation to the orientation of the Piso dies. Significant portions of both types are clearly discernible, and it includes the first two digits in the date for the Washington Quarter.

The United States Mint struck coins of several denominations for the Philippines during the 1970s, including the Piso. Examples of the KM-203 type were prepared solely with the dates 1972 and 1974, so it is likely that this error was created in one of those two years. A spectacular double denomination error, this piece combines two relatively large-denomination coins from two different countries.

Rarity: Unique
Value: $12,500

3.

Undated Coronet Large Cent
Overstruck on a Great Britain, 1731 Halfpenny, Spink-3717—PCGS VF-20

There is a tremendous amount of detail visible from the Halfpenny. In fact, the portraits of both Liberty and Britain's King George II are each clearly discernible even though they are nearly perfectly lined up on the obverse of the coin.

The portrait of Liberty on the obverse of the Coronet Cent is that used in the late 1830s before introduction of the Braided Hair type toward the end of 1839. That a British Halfpenny could have accidentally found its way into the Cent press in the United States Mint during this time period is not beyond the realm of possibility. Many foreign coins continued to circulate in the United States for several decades after the end of the Revolutionary War, and such pieces probably did not entirely disappear from commercial channels in this country until the mid-to-late 1850s. This important error is one of only two known for a U.S. Large Cent overstruck on a foreign coin.

Rarity: 2 Known
Value: $10,000

4.

Chile, 1836 8 Escudos, Fr-37

Overstruck on a Chile, Undated 8 Escudos, Fr-33—
ANACS AU-53

There is considerable detail remaining from the undertype including the sun and lettering on the obverse. Both sides are minimally worn and problem-free for the assigned grade.

The Fr-33 attribution is reserved for those Chilean 8 Escudos struck from 1818 through 1834, which is the type immediately preceding that of the 1836 Fr-37. In the 2006 book *Standard Catalog of World Coins: 1801-1900*, 5th Edition, the authors state that overstrike errors involving coins of these types are "rarely encountered."

Rarity: 5 Known
Value: $10,000

5.

France, 1701-C ½ Louis d'or, Type of Fr-437

Overstruck Off-center on a France, 1694 ½ Louis d'or, Fr-434—ANACS AU-50

A C mintmark on French coins denotes that they were struck in Caen. I contacted several well-known experts in world gold coinage and none of them have ever seen or heard rumor of a ½ Louis d'or struck in Caen with a 1701 date. This piece, therefore, could be a trial piece, pattern or presentation coin prepared using a reverse die with the C mintmark. Regardless of the exact circumstances under which this coin was prepared, the minters seem to have had difficulty procuring a blank planchet and, instead, decided to use a previously struck 1694 ½ Louis d'or.

Rarity: Unique
Value: $5,000

6.

Panama, 1982 ½ Balboa, KM-12b
Overstruck on a 1976 Bicentennial Kennedy Half Dollar—ANACS MS-63

Considerable detail from the undertype is still visible, including Kennedy's portrait and the date on the obverse as well as some of the lettering on the reverse.

This Choice Mint State example is a remarkable double denomination error that involves coins struck for two different countries with a six-year spread between the dates on the dies.

Rarity: Unknown
Value: $2,000

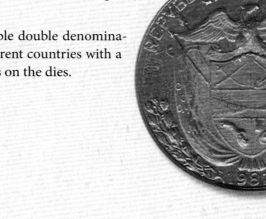

Price Guide for Overstrikes

Prices fluctuate due to the date, grade, eye appeal and how dramatic the striking error is. Rarity is also a factor. The price is sometimes based on the rarity and grade of the type of coin as well as how rare the error is. There is no price guide for this chapter because of the extreme rarity and low number of errors available.

Chapter 20

Partial Collars

Partial collar errors occur when there is a malfunction in the press that causes the collar to be in an incorrect position at the time of striking. The collar is a critical component of the modern minting process because it ensures a uniform shape and diameter to all coins being struck during a given press run. If a planchet is not properly seated in the collar, it will receive only partial reeding around the edge when it is struck by the dies.

The anvil die, which is usually the reverse, is recessed in the collar. After the coin is struck, the anvil die raises upward to eject the coin from the collar. Around the turn of the 21st century, the United States Mint installed new machinery which allows either the obverse or reverse die to be installed in the anvil position in the press.

1.

1875-CC Liberty Double Eagle
Partial Collar—NGC MS-62

A full partial collar error is easy to identify on this important Double Eagle, particularly because it is encapsulated in a special NGC holder that allows us to view the coin's edge.

This is an important piece, and for several reasons. First, major mint errors on gold coins are extremely rare coins. Second, this 1875-CC Double Eagle is one of only two major mint errors known on a United States gold coin struck in the Carson City Mint. Third, the Carson City Mint is one of the most popular coinage facilities in U.S. history, and it has a strong following among specialized gold collectors. Finally, the 1875-CC is a conditionally challenging Double Eagle even when properly struck, and only a couple of hundred Mint State examples are believed to have survived from an original mintage of 111,151 pieces (this estimate is per Douglas Winter and Jim Halperin, *Gold Coins of the Carson City Mint*, 2001).

Rarity: Unique
Value: $50,000

2.

1873 Open 3 Liberty Double Eagle
Misaligned Partial Collar—PCGS AU-58

A multiple mint error, the obverse die was misaligned in the press with the result that the obverse appears to be slightly off-center. Additionally, this coin was also struck with a partial collar, which in itself is a rare error on a large-denomination U.S. gold coin.

The 1873 Open is one of the most easily obtainable issues in the Type II Double Eagle series of 1866-1876. As a whole, however, this type is one of the most difficult to collect in all of U.S. numismatics, particularly in the finer circulated and Mint State grades.

Rarity: Unique
Value: $10,000

3.

1844-O Liberty Eagle

Partial Collar—AU-50

A full partial collar error, more than 50% of the reeding is missing completely around the edge of this coin.

The No Motto Liberty Eagle series from the New Orleans Mint has yielded only a few major mint errors of all kinds. As an issue, the 1844-O has a surviving population of only 250-300 coins in all grades (per Doug Winter, *Gold Coins of the New Orleans Mint: 1839-1909*, 2006), and the vast majority of those coins grade no higher than EF-45.

Rarity: Unique
Value: $7,500

4.

1900-S Liberty Double Eagle

Partial Collar—ANACS MS-60

This impressive error is a full partial collar that has the appearance of being broadstruck. It is another rare mint error on a large-denomination United States gold coin.

Rarity: 2 Known
Value: $7,500

Price Guide for Partial Collars

Denomination	XF/AU	Unc	Denomination	XF/AU	Unc
Large Cent	$100	$200	Barber Half	$1,000	$1,500
Flying Eagle Cent (1857–1858)	$500	$1,500	Walking Liberty Half	$1,500	$3,500
Indian Cent	$35	$100	Franklin Half	$500	$1,000
Lincoln Cent 1930 and Earlier	$30	$100	Kennedy Half Silver	$50	$100
Lincoln Cent 1943 Steel	$25	$50	Kennedy Half Clad	$20	$30
Proof Lincoln Cent	N/A	$750	Proof Clad Half	N/A	$2,000
3 Cent Nickel	$150	$500	Morgan Dollar	$150	$300
3 Cent Silver	$750	$2,000	Peace Dollar	$1,000	$2,500
Shield Nickel	$200	$600	Eisenhower Dollar	$50	$100
Liberty Nickel	$50	$150	Susan B Anthony Dollar	$20	$30
Buffalo Nickel	$50	$75	Sacagawea Dollar	N/A	$100
Jefferson Nickel War Time	$40	$60	Presidential Dollar	N/A	$250
Proof Jefferson Nickel	N/A	$1,000	$1 Gold Type I	$2,500	$5,000
Seated Half Dime Legend	$750	$1,500	$1 Gold Type 2	$5,000	$10,000
Seated Dime Legend	$500	$1,250	$1 Gold Type 3	$2,000	$3,000
Barber Dime	$75	$150	$2 ½ Liberty	$2,000	$3,000
Mercury Dime	$30	$100	$2 ½ Indian	$2,000	$3,000
Proof Clad Dime	N/A	$1,250	$3	$5,000	$10,000
Barber Quarter	$300	$750	$5 Liberty	$3,000	$5,000
Standing Liberty Quarter	$1,250	$2,000	$5 Indian	$4,000	$6,000
Washington Quarter Silver	$40	$75	$10 Liberty	$4,000	$7,500
State Quarter	N/A	$15	$10 Indian	$5,000	$7,500
Proof Clad Quarter	N/A	$1,500	$20 Liberty Type 3	$7,500	$10,000

Chapter 21

Proof Errors

*P*roof coins are struck by technicians who hand feed the blanks into special presses. They are produced, examined, and packaged using extreme quality control. It is very unusual to find major proof errors. A few broadstrikes, off-centers, double strikes in collars and off-metals have been known to be found in sealed proof sets. Proof errors are aggressively sought after by many error collectors.

A very small group of Proof errors recently came from a collection that was auctioned by the State of California. The U.S. Secret Service inspected and released this collection to the State of California determining that it was legal to own. The State of California then auctioned the collection and it has been dispersed since the sale.

1.

Undated Proof Eisenhower Dollar
Double Struck on an Aluminum Planchet—PCGS Proof-64 Cameo

2 grams. This proof Eisenhower Dollar was struck at the San Francisco Mint in the 1970s on an aluminum planchet that weighs only 2 grams. The coin is also double struck with a few degrees rotation between impressions. Both strikes are well centered and, while the peripheral devices are largely off the planchet, the central devices are fully intact. Additionally, both Eisenhower's portrait on the obverse and the reverse eagle exhibit an overlay of mint frost that contrasts nicely with a mirrored finish in the fields.

There are only a few Mint errors in the entire U.S. coinage family that involve aluminum planchets. This Eisenhower Dollar is one of the most spectacular errors attributed to the modern U.S. Mint.

Rarity: 2 Known
Value: $30,000

2.

Proof 1973-S Eisenhower Dollar
Struck on a Half Dollar Planchet—PCGS Proof-64

The dies were flush with the lower-obverse and upper-obverse edges of the planchet, with the result that the peripheral devices in the opposite areas on both sides are off the planchet. On the positive side, the obverse clearly shows Eisenhower's portrait, the date and the S mintmark. On the reverse, the Latin motto E PLURIBUS UNUM, the moon and the eagle are all fully detailed.

There are only a handful of wrong planchet errors attributed to the proof Eisenhower Dollar series of 1973-1978.

Ex: Private Mint Error Collection (formed in the 1970s).

Rarity: 3-5 Known
Value: $20,000

3.

Proof 1973-S Kennedy Half Dollar
Overstruck on an Aluminum Token—PCGS Proof-65 Cameo

The token is essentially the same size as a regular proof Kennedy Half Dollar, and both sides of this error display full definition to the Kennedy Half Dollar design.

There are only a few overstrike errors on U.S. proof coins that involve aluminum tokens, and the present example is unique for the Half Dollar denomination.

Rarity: Unique
Value: $10,000

4.

Proof 1875 Three-Cent Nickel
Double Struck—PCGS Proof-64

PCGS has certified this piece as being double struck in the collar with a 10% rotation between strikes. Detail from both strikes is easily discernible, giving the coin a very dramatic appearance.

Major mint errors on 19th century proof coins of any denomination are seldom encountered. The proof 1875 Three-Cent Nickel has a limited mintage when compared to, say a proof Lincoln Cent or Jefferson Nickel from the mid-to-late 20th century. The exact number of proof Three-Cent Nickels struck in 1875 is unknown, but the 2008 edition of *A Guide Book of United States Coins* by R.S. Yeoman provides an estimate mintage of 700+ pieces.

Rarity: Unique
Value: $7,500

5.

Undated Proof 40% Silver Kennedy Half Dollar
Struck on a Dime Planchet—PCGS Proof-66

This proof Kennedy Half should have been struck on a 40% Silver Proof Half Dollar Planchet. Instead, it is struck on a copper-nickel clad planchet intended for a proof Roosevelt Dime. The reverse is particularly dramatic with much of the eagle present.

Rarity: 3 Known
Value: $7,500

6.

Proof 1968-S Kennedy Half Dollar

Struck on a Philippines, 50 Sentimos Planchet—ANACS Proof-63

This proof Kennedy Half Dollar error is struck on a full-size Philippine aluminum 50 Sentimos planchet. The first coins of this type were struck in 1967 (the attribution is KM-200), so this planchet was probably leftover from that issue.

A very small group of Proof errors recently came from a collection that was auctioned by the State of California. The U.S. Secret Service inspected and released this collection to the State of California determining that it was legal to own. The State of California then auctioned the collection and it has been dispersed since the sale.

Rarity: Unique
Value: $7,500

7.

Proof 1970-S Roosevelt Dime

Struck on a Nepal, 2 Paisa Planchet—ANACS Proof-63

This incredible mint error is a proof 1970-S Roosevelt Dime struck on an aluminum planchet that was originally intended for a Nepal proof 2 Paisa.

There are only a handful of wrong planchet Dime errors known, and this piece is even more significant since the United States Mint has never produced any regular-issue coins in aluminum.

Rarity: 2 Known
Value: $7,500

8.

Proof 1981-S Washington Quarter

Double Struck Off-Center—ANACS Proof-65 Heavy Cameo

Both strikes are approximately 5-10% off-center, and they occurred out of the collar with the result that the planchet expanded in size and eventually cracked. The first strike is readily discernible as partial detail to Washington's portrait on the obverse and the eagle and lettering on the reverse.

Rarity: Unique
Value: $7,500

9.

Proof 1972-S Washington Quarter

Multi-Struck Reverse Die Cap—ANACS Proof-65

This proof Washington Quarter is a die cap that adhered to the reverse die. The coin is struck multiple times with detail from several impressions visible on the obverse around Washington's portrait and the digits in the date.

Rarity: Unique
Value: $6,000

10.

Proof 1968-S Washington Quarter

Struck on a Dime Planchet—PCGS Proof-63

This proof Quarter is struck on a clad Dime planchet in error. Both sides are relatively well centered on the planchet, and the obverse detail includes a bold S mintmark and most of the date.

Rarity: 5 Known
Value: $6,000

11.

Undated Proof Jefferson Nickel

Double Struck—ANACS Proof-65

The first strike was properly positioned on the planchet, but the second produced a uniface double-struck error on the obverse. The second strike is approximately 40% off center between 4 and 5 o'clock. This impression does not include the date area, and it also obscured the date area from the first strike. On the other hand, the second strike is positioned in such a way that considerable portions of two obverse portraits are clearly visible.

Rarity: Unique
Value: $6,000

12.

Proof 1968-S Lincoln Cent
Struck on a Dime Planchet—ANACS Proof-65

This wrong planchet error was created when a copper-nickel clad Dime planchet was fed into a press that was set up to strike proof 1968-S Lincoln Cents.

Rarity: 10 Known
Value: $2,500

Price Guide for Proof Errors

Denomination	Broadstrikes	Die Trials	Double/Triple Strikes	Off-Center Strikes	Partial Collar Errors
Proof Lincoln Cent	$1,500 - $2,500	$1,000	$4,000	$1,500 - $3,000	$500
Proof Jefferson Nickel	$2,500 - $4,000	$4,000	$6,000	$2,000 - $5,000	$1,000
Proof Clad Dime	$3,000 - $5,000	$4,000	$6,000	$2,500 - $5,000	$1,250
Proof Clad Quarter	$4,000 - $5,000	$5,000	$10,000	$7,500	$1,500
Proof Clad Half	$5,000 - $7,000	$4,000 - $5,000	$10,000	$10,000	$2,000
Proof Eisenhower	$15,000	-	$25,000	-	$4,000
Presidential Dollar	-	-	-	-	1 Known (Madison)

Chapter 22

Proof Pattern Errors

P roof mint errors on U.S. patterns are even rarer than on modern U.S. coinage. Proof coins are struck twice by technicians who hand feed the blanks into special presses. They are produced, examined, and packaged using extreme quality control. Mint errors on patterns are rare since the mintages are considerably less than on modern coinage. The only proof pattern mint error that is occasionally found are double strikes with a slight rotation between the strikes. Broadstrikes, off-centers and off-metals are extremely rare. These mint errors are sought after by both collectors of patterns and mint errors.

1.

Pattern 1846 Liberty Half Eagle, Judd-110a

Unique—Overstruck on a Pattern 1846 Liberty Quarter Eagle—
NGC MS-65

A unique and famous pattern, this piece is actually a copper die trial striking of the 1846 Liberty Quarter Eagle with the reverse overstruck by an obverse die for the 1846 Liberty Half Eagle.

This coin is the only pattern of any denomination struck in the United States Mint during the decade from 1840 through 1849. It has a long and distinguished pedigree in the numismatic market, and was described in the catalog for the 1952 ANA Convention sale as follows:

The obverse of an 1846 half eagle struck upon the reverse of an 1846 quarter eagle. A clear and intentional overstrike, and not the combination of two obverse dies. The reverse (obverse of the quarter eagle) shows plainly the effect of the half eagle impression. The planchet is somewhat irregular due to the lack of a collar during the second operation...Assuredly a Mint product...The first we have seen or heard of.

Ex: 1952 ANA Sale (New Netherlands, 8/1952), lot 4478.

Rarity: Unique
Value: $100,000

2.

Pattern 1873 Closed 3 Liberty Double Eagle, Judd-1344

Double Struck—NGC Proof-61 Red and Brown

Regular die trial striking of the 1873 Closed 3 Double Eagle. Struck in copper with a reeded edge.

This error was double struck in the collar with noticeable rotation between the two impressions. Considerable detail from the first strike is visible on the obverse around the stars, date and Liberty's portrait. On the reverse, remnants of the first strike are discernible around the eagle, the legend UNITED STATES OF AMERICA and the denomination TWENTY D.

In addition to its importance as a major Mint error, this pattern is a major rarity in an absolute sense. In fact, PCGS and NGC combined have certified only three examples of Judd-1344 as of March 2008. One of the certified coins has been gilt, or plated in gold.

Rarity: 2 Known
Value: $40,000

3.

Pattern 1869 Three-Cent Silver, Judd-682

Obverse Double Struck—PCGS Proof-64 Cameo

A regular die trial striking of the 1869 Three-Cent Silver. Struck in aluminum with a plain edge.

There is substantial rotation between the strikes that is most dramatic around the star.

Whether we view this piece as a pattern or a proof Three-Cent Silver, it emerges as a leading rarity in the market for major U.S. Mint errors. Judd-682 is also a significant numismatic rarity in its own right with perhaps just four-to-six specimens known.

Rarity: Unique
Value: $20,000

4.

Pattern 1871 Standard Silver Dollar, Judd-1133

Double Struck—PCGS Proof-63

The obverse depicts Chief Engraver Longacre's Indian Princess design, while the reverse exhibits the denomination 1 DOLLAR within a cotton and corn, with the word STANDARD above. Struck in silver with a reeded edge.

This pattern Standard Dollar was double struck in the collar with a five-degree rotation between impressions.

Rarity: 2 Known
Value: $10,000

Price Guide for Proof Pattern Errors

Prices fluctuate due to the date, grade, eye appeal and how dramatic the striking error is. Rarity is also a factor. The price is sometimes based on the rarity and grade of the type of coin as well as how rare the error is. There is no price guide for this chapter because of the extreme rarity and low number of errors available.

Chapter 23

Proof Planchet Errors

*T*his type of error has only occurred on modern coinage. The Philadelphia Mint prepares the proof planchets which are then sent to San Francisco or West Point for striking. When few proof planchets accidentally mix in with the regular blanks, they can be struck by regular dies. Several 1999 Susan B Anthony dollars have shown up that are either broadstruck or off-center on proof planchets, but struck by regular dies. These coins have extreme proof-like fields and a pitted appearance on the unstruck portion of the blank. These are the characteristics that distinguish this rare and unusual type of mint error.

1.

1999-P Susan B. Anthony Dollar
Struck 35% Off-Center on a Proof Planchet—NGC MS-65

This error occurred when a few proof planchets were inadvertently mixed with regular planchets intended for the production of business strike 1999-P Anthony Dollars. One of these planchets was then struck 35% off-center at 4 o'clock.

I know of only four 1999-P Anthony Dollars that are struck off center on proof planchets.

Rarity: 4 Known
Value: $7,500

2.

1999-P Susan B. Anthony Dollar

Double Struck—PCGS MS-65

This is an intriguing wrong planchet error, because the Mint intended that 1999-P Anthony Dollar dies be used solely in the production of business strike coins. The present example, however, is struck on a specially prepared, highly polished proof planchet. This coin is also double struck with the second impression approximately 40% off center between 6 and 7 o'clock. The second impression is die struck only on the obverse, where part of the date is visible at the lower border. The pressure that the dies exerted on the planchet during creation of this error caused it to expand and eventually split at the left and right borders.

Interestingly, several of the Anthony Dollar errors that are struck on proof planchets are also double struck, broadstruck or off-center.

Rarity: 5 Known
Value: $5,000

3.

1999-P Susan B. Anthony Dollar

Struck Four Times on a Proof Planchet—ANACS MS-64

This wrong planchet error was struck four times out of the collar, thus explaining the greatly expanded size of the planchet. Such was the pressure that the multiple impressions exerted on the planchet that it eventually cracked at the right-obverse border.

Rarity: 5 Known
Value: $3,000

4.

1969-S Lincoln Cent
Struck on a Proof Dime Planchet—PCGS MS-60

The San Francisco Mint struck both proof and business strike Cents in 1969. This piece was struck from non-polished dies that were intended for use in the production of business strikes. On the other hand, the planchet was specially prepared and was supposed to be used in the production of proof Dimes, probably the 1969-S Roosevelt issue. Most of the detail is visible on the obverse and, on the reverse, only the tops of the letters in the words UNITED and STATES are off the planchet.

Rarity: 10 Known
Value: $2,500

Price Guide for Proof Planchet Errors

Prices fluctuate due to the date, grade, eye appeal and how dramatic the striking error is. Rarity is also a factor. The price is sometimes based on the rarity and grade of the type of coin as well as how rare the error is. There is no price guide for this chapter because of the extreme rarity and low number of errors available.

Chapter 24

Spectacular Errors

A spectacular error can be anything. Many factors have to come together for a mint error to be truly spectacular. An example is a Susan B Anthony dollar struck on a Sacagawea dollar brass planchet or a Sacagawea dollar struck on a Susan B Anthony dollar clad planchet. Some other examples include coins that are struck and bonded together, coins struck on feeder fingers and coins struck over tokens or foreign coins.

1.

1884-CC Morgan Silver Dollar

Split Planchet—PCGS MS-64

This 1884-CC Silver Dollar is struck on a planchet that was not properly produced and included impurities in the alloy. The stress of striking caused the planchet to split in half nearly horizontally through the center of the coin. Amazingly, this error survived intact and both halves of the planchet still fit snugly together.

One of the most dramatic Morgan Dollar errors known, this "Broken CC" is also significant because it is a product of the Carson City Mint. Due both to its association with the Old West and the unique double mintmark of its coins, the Carson City Mint is one of the most romanticized and popular coinage facilities in U.S. history.

Rarity: Unique
Value: $50,000

2.

1920 Buffalo Nickel
Struck on a (Full Size) Copper Planchet—NGC AU-55

89% copper, 8% zinc, 3% tin. 4.96 grams, or 76.54 grains. Truly an amazing mint error, this piece is struck on a copper planchet that has the same diameter, thickness and weight of a normal Buffalo Nickel planchet.

Buffalo Nickels struck on bronze Cent planchets are very scarce, while those struck on 90% silver dime planchet are extremely rare. Struck on a full-size copper planchet, the present example is unique, and was featured on the front page of the November 19th, 2001 issue of *Coin World*.

Rarity: Unique
Value: $40,000

3.

1818/5 Capped Bust Quarter, B-1, Rarity-3 (as a Die Pair)
Struck 5% Off-Center—NGC MS-65

The strike is 5% off-center at 11 o'clock, with the result that only the tops of a few letters in the word UNITED and the tips of the olive leaves are off the planchet on the reverse. All devices on the obverse are present.

Any major mint error in the Capped Bust Quarter series is an extremely rare coin. This particular example is of further significance both because it is an example of the Large Size Bust Quarter type of 1815-1828 and because it is an overdate. A lovely Gem, both sides possess richly original toning to the surfaces.

Rarity: Unique
Value: $40,000

4.

1920 Buffalo Nickel

Struck 40% Off-Center on a Cent Planchet—PCGS MS-64 Brown

A multiple mint error, this Buffalo Nickel is struck 40% off center on a Cent planchet.

One of the most spectacular major mint errors of all time, the combination of wrong planchet and off-center errors would make this coin a centerpiece of any error collection. The eye appeal is simply extraordinary!

Rarity: Unique
Value: $40,000

5.

Undated Eisenhower Dollar

Double Struck on a Dime Planchet—PCGS MS-64

The second strike is 80% off center and die struck on both sides. The most dramatic detail is present on the reverse, where we can see the eagle's legs and tail, as well as most of the olive branch and the word DOLLAR.

Ex: Private Mint Error Collection (formed in the 1970s).

Rarity: Unique
Value: $35,000

6.

1999-P Susan B. Anthony Dollar
Broadstruck on a Sacagawea Dollar Planchet—PCGS MS-67

Another multiple mint error on an Anthony Dollar, this 1999-P is broadstruck out of the collar on a planchet intended for use in 2000 with the introduction of the Dollar series. As such, it is also a transitional error.

Rarity: Unique
Value: $25,000

7.

1943-S Lincoln Cent
Struck 15% Off-Center on a Dime Planchet—NGC AU-55

A spectacular multiple mint error, this 1943-S Cent is struck 15% off-center at 7 o'clock on a 90% silver Dime planchet.

Nearly in the Mint State category, this important mint error was produced the same year as the fabled 1943 "Copper" Cents.

Rarity: Unique
Value: $15,000

8.

Undated Statehood Quarter

Struck 50% Off-Center, Reverse Brockage on a Double Struck Jefferson Nickel on a Cent Planchet—ANACS MS-62

One of the most challenging, yet fascinating errors that I have ever encountered, this piece began its transformation into a major mint error when a Cent planchet was accidentally fed into a Nickel press. After being struck from the Jefferson Nickel dies, the planchet then found its way into a Statehood Quarter press where it was struck 50% off center at 4 o'clock. The reverse impression from in the Quarter press is a brockage of the obverse design showing part of Washington's portrait in mirror image. Additionally, the planchet rotated nearly 180 degrees counterclockwise between the Nickel strike and the Quarter strike, although it did not flipover.

This error may be even more intriguing that it already is since some experts believe that there is evidence of the planchet first having been struck from Lincoln Cent dies. If so, then this error would qualify as a triple denomination and not "just" a double denomination and a wrong planchet error.

Rarity: Unique
Value: $15,000

9.

2000-P Massachusetts Statehood Quarter

Overstruck on a 1999-P Georgia Statehood Quarter—ANACS MS-64

This Statehood Quarter Mint is both a dual-date (1999 and 2000) and "dual-state" (Georgia and Massachusetts) error. The latter type of error was actually unknown in the numismatic market until the discovery of this piece. The coin was found in circulation by a woman who was purposefully sorting through Statehood Quarters looking for significant mint errors.

Rarity: Unique
Value: $15,000

10.

France, 1831 5 Francs, Dav-89

Double Struck on a Brass Spoon—As Struck

27.8 grams. One of the most exotic mint errors that I have ever encountered, this piece is an 1831 French 5 Francs double struck on a brass spoon. Most of the detail from both the obverse and reverse dies is clearly visible, and part of the handle of the spoon is still attached. In the 1830s, wooden handles were attached to a notch on brass spoons just like this one.

Why or under what circumstances this intriguing piece was created is among the most intriguing questions in the error coin market of the 21st century.

Rarity: Unique
Value: $15,000

11.

Canada, 1978 Cent, KM-59.1

Multiple Overstrike on a Canada, 1974 Commemorative
10 Dollars, 1976 Montreal Olympics, KM-94—As Struck

A fascinating error, this Canadian 1974 Commemorative 10 Dollars was overstruck multiple times by dies for the 1978 Canadian Cent.

This is the most dramatic major Mint error on a Canadian coin that I have ever seen or handled. Not only did the planchet emerge from the Cent press without having suffered significant damage, but it has also managed to survive as struck since 1978.

Rarity: Unique
Value: $15,000

12.

1983-P Washington Quarter
Overstruck on a Brass Arcade Token—NGC MS-65

There is considerable detail remaining from the undertype, including the inscription THIS IS MY LUCKY DAY on the obverse.

A unique and spectacular error, I am at a loss to explain exactly how this piece was produced. How a brass arcade token found its way into a tote bin filled with copper-nickel clad Quarter planchets is anyone's guess.

Rarity: Unique
Value: $15,000

13.

Undated Washington Quarter
Multi Struck on a Pure Copper Core—PCGS MS-63

This piece is multi struck, uniface, on a pure copper core—the only such error known from the entire United States Quarter series. The multiple impressions have caused the planchet to expand to the size of a Half Dollar, and it has also developed several sizeable cracks at the rim. The edge is reeded.

Rarity: Unique
Value: $7,500

Price Guide for Spectacular Errors

Prices fluctuate due to the date, grade, eye appeal and how dramatic the striking error is. Rarity is also a factor. The price is sometimes based on the rarity and grade of the type of coin as well as how rare the error is. There is no price guide for this chapter because of the extreme rarity and low number of errors available.

Chapter 25

Fragments & Scraps

The blanking press takes the coils of metal strips and punches blanks out of it, ejecting the webbing at the other end. The webbing is cut into small scrap pieces to be melted and recycled. Occasionally a scrap piece will be mixed with the blank planchets and struck by the dies. Struck fragments are rare in the larger denominations. These can be uniface or die struck on both sides and are very rare on type coins.

1.

Undated Kennedy Half Dollar
Multi Struck on Scrap—NGC MS-65

Combing multiple major mint errors, this piece is struck several times on a piece of scrap. The force generated by the multiple impressions has caused the planchet to expand to nearly the size of a Morgan Silver Dollar. The second strike on the obverse is uniface.

Rarity: 10 Known
Value: $2,500

2.

1979-P Susan B. Anthony Dollar
Struck on Scrap—PCGS MS-66

0.51 grains. The weight of this error is less than half that of a normal Anthony Dollar planchet. The strike is rather nicely positioned on the scrap with half of both the obverse and reverse designs visible. The detail on the obverse even includes the final two digits in the date.

Rarity: 5 Known
Value: $1,250

3.

1972-Dated Washington Quarter
Struck on a Fragment—ANACS MS-62

The fragment upon which this error is struck has given it the look of a slightly off-center, elliptical clipped planchet error. This piece is die struck on both sides of the scrap and includes substantial amounts of the central definition. Most of the date is visible at the lower-obverse edge, but the mintmark area is obscured so I cannot determine if this piece was struck in the Philadelphia or Denver Mints.

Rarity: 20 Known
Value: $300

4.

Undated Lincoln Cent
Struck on a Fragment—ANACS MS-63 Red

Struck on a copper-plated zinc fragment, this piece does exhibit the first three digits 199 in the date. It is die struck on both sides and is as thin as a piece of paper. Importantly, this error is not struck on a split-off portion of a planchet. There are no striations on either side, which would indicate which side split off from the planchet, and the devices are fully struck on both sides. An error struck on a piece of a split-off planchet would usually be softly defined on one side.

Rarity: 20 Known
Value: $250

Price Guide for Fragments and Scraps

Denomination	Uniface	Die Struck Both Sides
Indian Cent	$1,000	$2,000
Lincoln Cent Wheat Ears	$750	$2,000
Lincoln Cent Memorial	$75	$125
3 Cent Nickel	$3,000	$3,500
Jefferson Nickel	$100	$200
Roosevelt Dime Silver	$500	$1,000
Roosevelt Dime Clad	$150	$250
Washington Quarter Silver	$1,000	$1,500
Washington Quarter Clad	$200	$300
State Quarter	$750	$1,000
Kennedy Half Silver	$1,500	$2,500
Kennedy Half Clad	$750	$1,250
Eisenhower Dollar	$2,000	$5,000
Susan B Anthony Dollar	$2,000	$3,000
Sacagawea Dollar	--	--

Chapter 26

Transitional Errors

A transitional error occurs when a coin is struck on a planchet from a previous year with different metal composition. The most famous transitional is a 1943 copper cent struck on a 1942 copper blank. 1943 cents were struck in steel because of the copper shortage during World War II. Other famous transitionals include 1965 coinage struck in silver instead of clad.

There are also transitionals struck on blanks for the next year. An example is 1964 coinage in clad instead of silver. Most recently, transitionals were discovered involving the Susan B Anthony and Sacagawea Dollars of 1999 and 2000. There are eight known 1999 Susan B Anthony Dollars struck on the brass planchet or the 2000 Sacagawea Dollar, and four known 2000 Sacagawea Dollars struck on a clad planchet for the 1999 Susan B Anthony Dollar.

1.

1943 Lincoln Cent
Struck on a Bronze Planchet—ANACS MS-61 Red and Brown

This is the world-famous 1943 "Copper" Cent, which many numismatists consider to be the "King of Mint Errors." This coin is a transitional error struck on a leftover bronze planchet from the Mint's production of 1942 Lincoln Cents. Although the government switched over to zinc-plated steel planchets for the production of Cents in 1943 (copper, a component of the bronze alloy, being a critical component for the production of certain weapons systems used in World War II), a few bronze planchets from the previous year remained in the tote bins that transported new planchets to the coining presses. These leftover bronze planchets eventually worked themselves loose from the inside of the tote bins and found their way into the press, where they were struck from 1943-dated dies.

1943 Cents struck on bronze planchets are known from all three United States Mints that were operational that year. I am aware of 14 examples of the 1943-P Bronze Cent, four examples of the 1943-S Bronze Cent and just one example of the 1943-D Bronze Cent. Auction prices realized for some of these errors from the late 1990s and early years of the 21st century range from $75,000 to $200,000.

Rarity: 20 Known
Value: $200,000

2.

2000-P Sacagawea Dollar
Struck on a Susan B. Anthony Dollar Planchet—PCGS MS-68

Instead of being struck in the brass composition approved for the Sacagawea Dollar, the Mint accidentally struck this coin on a leftover copper-nickel clad planchet intended for an Anthony Dollar.

This important modern U.S. Mint error was featured on the front page of the May 22nd, 2000 issue of *Coin World*.

Rarity: 5 Known
Value: $17,500

3.

1999-P Susan B. Anthony Dollar
Struck on a Sacagawea Dollar Planchet—PCGS MS-66

Along with the 90% silver and copper-nickel clad errors of 1964/1965, the Anthony and Sacagawea Dollar errors of 1999/2000 are the most significant transitional errors discovered during the second half of the 20th century.

Rarity: 10 Known
Value: $15,000

4.

1964 Kennedy Half Dollar
Struck on a Copper-Nickel Clad Quarter Planchet—PCGS MS-65

Instead of being struck on a 90% silver, 10% copper planchet as intended for the 1964 Kennedy Half Dollar, this transitional error is struck on a copper-nickel clad planchet intended for a 1965 Washington Quarter. The strike is well centered on both sides, although the size difference between the Quarter planchet and the Half Dollar dies has resulted in many of the peripheral devices being off the planchet. The tops of most digits in the date, however, are still discernible at the lower-obverse border.

Rarity: 5 Known
Value: $10,000

5.

1944-P Wartime Jefferson Nickel
Struck on a Copper-Nickel Planchet—PCGS VF-25

Beginning in 1942 and continuing through the end of 1945, the United States Mint struck Jefferson Nickels in a wartime alloy of 56% copper, 35% silver and 9% manganese. Notably absent from this alloy is nickel, which the federal government deemed a critical resource in the production of weapons and munitions needed to fight World War II. To distinguish these Wartime Nickels from their counterparts in the earlier and later Jefferson Nickel series, a large mintmark was placed on the reverse above the dome of Monticello.

The error pictured here was accidentally struck on a leftover copper-nickel planchet from the early Jefferson Nickel series of 1938-1942. The use of this planchet to strike a 1944-P Nickel obviously escaped the attention of the contemporary public as the coin has acquired considerable wear from what appears to be years spent in circulation. Fortunately, it was eventually recognized as a major Mint error and has since been preserved in problem-free VF condition.

Rarity: 5 Known
Value: $10,000

6.

1965 Washington Quarter
Struck on a 90% Silver Planchet—ANACS AU-50

This 1965 Quarter is struck on a 90% silver Quarter planchet leftover from the Mint's production of Quarters in 1964. All 1965 Quarters were supposed to have been struck on the new copper-nickel clad planchets. Those that were not, such as the present example, are among the most significant transitional errors in U.S. Mint history.

Rarity: 20 Known
Value: $7,500

7.

1965 Roosevelt Dime
Struck on a 90% Silver Planchet—ANACS AU-55

Like the 1965 Washington Quarter below, this 1965 Roosevelt Dime is a transitional error struck on a 90% silver planchet intended for use in 1964. This coin should have been struck on a new copper-nickel clad planchet that the Mint introduced for regular-issue production in 1965.

Rarity: 20 Known
Value: $7,500

8.

1983-P Jefferson Nickel
Struck on a Bronze Cent Planchet—PCGS MS-65 Red

3.1 grams. This extremely rare 1983 Jefferson Nickel transitional error is struck on a bronze Cent planchet that weighs 3.1 grams. These planchets were used to strike Lincoln Cents prior to 1983, the Mint adopting a new copper-plated zinc planchet weighing 2.5 grams in 1982.

Rarity: 2 Known
Value: $5,000

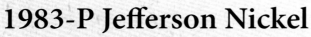

9.

1989-D Lincoln Cent
Double Struck on a Bronze Planchet—ICG MS-63 Red and Brown

This transitional error is struck on a bronze planchet leftover from the Mint's production of Cents prior to 1983. The Mint was supposed to use copper-plated zinc planchets to strike all 1989-D Lincoln Cents. This coin was also double struck in the collar with considerable rotation between the strikes.

Rarity: Unique
Value: $5,000

10.

1989-D Lincoln Cent
Struck on a Bronze Planchet—ANACS MS-64 Red

This transitional Mint error was struck in the Denver Mint during 1989 on a pre-1983 bronze Cent planchet. As stated above, all 1989-D Cents were supposed to have been struck on copper-plated zinc planchets.

Rarity: Unique
Value: $3,000

Price Guide for Transitional Errors

Denomination	Off-Metal Planchet	Circulated	AU	Unc	Choice Unc–Gem
Lincoln Cent 1943 Transitional	Copper Cent Planchet	$75,000	$100,000	$200,000	$250,000
Lincoln Cent 1944 Transitional	Steel Cent Planchet	$30,000	$50,000	$100,000	$150,000
Lincoln Cent 1964 Transitional	Clad Dime Planchet	$2,500	$4,000	$5,000	$6,500
Lincoln Cent 1965 Transitional	Silver Dime Planchet	$2,750	$4,500	$6,000	$7,500
Roosevelt Dime 1964 Transitional	Clad Dime Planchet	$5,000	$6,500	$7,500	$8,500
Roosevelt Dime 1965 Transitional	Silver Dime Planchet	$5,000	$6,500	$7,500	$8,500
Washington Quarter 1964 Transitional	Clad Quarter Planchet	$5,000	$6,500	$7,500	$8,500
Washington Quarter 1965 Transitional	Silver Quarter Planchet	$5,000	$6,500	$7,500	$8,500
Kennedy Half 1964 Transitional	Clad Half Planchet	$5,000	$6,000	$7,000	$9,000
Kennedy Half 1965 Transitional	Silver Half Planchet	$5,000	$6,500	$7,500	$10,000
Kennedy Half 1964 Transitional	Clad Quarter Planchet	$5,000	$6,000	$7,500	$8,500
Kennedy Half 1965 Transitional	Silver Quarter Planchet	$6,000	$7,500	$8,000	$9,000
Eisenhower Dollar Transitional	40% Silver Planchet	$2,750	$3,000	$3,500	$4,000
Susan B Anthony Dollar Transitional	Sacagawea Planchet	N/A	N/A	$12,500	$15,000
Sacagawea Dollar Transitional	Susan B Anthony Planchet	N/A	N/A	$12,500	$15,000

Chapter 27

Two-Headed &
Two-Tailed Errors

*A*s their name implies, "two-headed" and "two-tailed" coins are errors that are struck with two obverse or two reverse dies, respectively. As of 2007, PCGS , NGC and ANACS have authenticated and certified approximately 50 genuine errors of this type. Only four of these coins were struck in the United States Mint: three Quarters and one Dime.

1.

European Economic Community, Five-Piece Euro Set

Struck with Two Reverse Dies—ANACS-Certified

Since each coin in this set was struck with two reverse dies, and since 12 member states of the European Economic Community all use the same reverse design for these coins, it is impossible to determine the country of origin for these errors.

Mike Faraone, a grader at PCGS and formerly with ANACS, states that this set is, "one of the most exciting mint error discoveries that I've ever examined and authenticated at ANACS." He also believes that, "it is amazing that these new Euro coins were all struck by two reverse dies." This is one of the most exotic dramatic and unique mint error discoveries of the 21st century.

Rarity: 2 Known
Value: $15,000

First Coin in Set:

European Economic Community, Undated Euro 20 Cents Reverse Muled with a Euro 50 Cents Reverse

MS-65 (ANACS)

Unlike the other coins in this set, the present example was not only struck from two reverse dies, but it is a mule of two different Euro denominations.

Second Coin in Set:

European Economic Community, Undated Euro Cent—Struck with Two Reverse Dies
MS-64 Red (ANACS)

Third Coin in Set:

European Economic Community, Undated Euro 5 Cents—Struck with Two Reverse Dies
MS-62 Red (ANACS)

Fourth Coin in Set:

European Economic Community, Undated Euro 20 Cents—Struck with Two Reverse Dies
MS-65 (ANACS)

Fifth Coin in Set:

European Economic Community, Undated Euro 50 Cents—Struck with Two Reverse Dies
MS-64 (ANACS)

2.

Canada, 1978 Cent, KM-59.1

Struck with Two Reverse Dies, Die Cap—PCGS MS-64 Red and Brown

This Canadian Cent is the only "two-headed" or "two-tailed" error that is also a die cap.

I have handled most of the world coins that were struck with either two obverse or two reverse dies and subsequently submitted to PCGS for authentication. Two of those coins are two-tailed Canadian Cents that were featured in a front page article in *Coin World* on October 1st, 2001.

Ex: Private Collection of Canadian Mint Errors.

Rarity: Unique
Value: $15,000

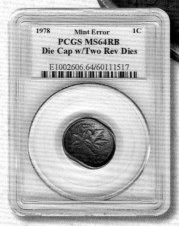

3.

Great Britain, 1971 Halfpenny, Spink-4239

Struck with Two Obverse Dies on a Copper-Nickel Planchet—NGC MS-61

In addition to being struck with two obverse dies, this error is struck on a copper-nickel planchet instead of a bronze planchet. As far as I know, it is the only double error of this kind—a two-headed off metal!

Rarity: Unique
Value: $15,000

Price Guide for Two-Headed & Two-Tailed Coins

Prices fluctuate due to the date, grade, eye appeal and how dramatic the striking error is. Rarity is also a factor. The price is sometimes based on the rarity and grade of the type of coin as well as how rare the error is. There is no price guide for this chapter because of the extreme rarity and low number of errors available.

Chapter 28

Uniface Strikes

*U*niface coins are the result of two blank planchets entering the press at the same time. During striking, one of the planchet obstructs the other and prevents it from receiving an impression from one of the dies.

There are many different variations of uniface errors. In addition to coins with a completely blank obverse or reverse, I have seen some uniface errors on off-center coins. There are also mated pairs involving a uniface error, as well as uniface errors struck from a capped die.

1.

Undated (1850) Pattern Three-Cent Silver, Judd-125 Original

Uniface Strike—ANACS Proof-60

The reverse is sharply struck, but the obverse is blank since that side of the coin was struck against a blank planchet that capped the obverse die. Although the nonexistent obverse design included the date, the reverse design attributes this piece as Judd-125 and, by extension, confirms that this error was struck in 1850.

All major mint errors on pattern coins are exceedingly rare. This piece is also significant because it is an early pattern of the Three-Cent Silver type—a denomination that has yielded very few errors even from the regular-issue series of 1851-1873.

Ex: Bolt Collection; Numismatics Ltd.

Rarity: Unique
Value: $12,500

2.

Undated Three-Cent Nickel

Struck Through Late Stage Cap Die—NGC AU-53

This Three-Cent Nickel was struck through an obverse die cap.

Major mint errors on 19th century U.S. type coins of all denominations are very scarce, while those attributed to the Three-Cent Nickel series of 1865-1889 are nothing short of rare.

Rarity: 5 Known
Value: $3,500

3.

1907 Indian Cent
Uniface Strike—NGC AU-50 Brown

This uniface Indian Cent was either struck through a reverse die cap or two planchets became stuck together and were fed into the press at the same time.

Rarity: 20 Known
Value: $750

4.

Undated Washington Quarter
Uniface Strike on a Dime Planchet—ANACS MS-60

This Washington Quarter is struck on a copper-nickel clad planchet intended for a Roosevelt Dime. It is also uniface since the obverse was resting against a blank (probably Quarter) planchet. The Dime planchet expanded in the press, and the only major design element that is missing from the reverse is the denomination QUARTER DOLLAR.

Rarity: 20 Known
Value: $500

Price Guide for Uniface Strikes

Denomination	Uniface Obverse XF	Uniface Obverse Unc	Uniface Reverse XF	Uniface Reverse Unc
Large Cent	$1,500	$4,000	$1,250	$2,000
Indian Cent	$1,250	$3,000	$1,000	$2,500
Lincoln Cent 1943 Steel	$250	$500	$200	$400
Lincoln Cent Wheat Ears	$50	$100	$40	$75
3 Cent Nickel	$1,500	$3,000	$1,250	$2,500
Shield Nickel	$1,750	$4,000	$1,500	$3,000
Liberty Nickel	$2,000	$3,500	$1,500	$3,000
Buffalo Nickel	$2,250	$3,000	$2,000	$2,500
Jefferson Nickel War Time	$300	$750	$250	$500
Jefferson Nickel	$20	$40	$20	$40
Barber Dime	$2,000	$3,000	$1,500	$2,500
Mercury Dime	$1,500	$2,500	$1,250	$2,250
Roosevelt Dime Silver	$100	$150	$100	$150
Roosevelt Dime Clad	$40	$75	$35	$60
Washington Quarter Silver	$400	$750	$350	$500
Washington Quarter Clad	$100	$125	$75	$100
State Quarter	N/A	$300	N/A	$500
Kennedy Half Clad	$750	$1,000	$500	$750
Eisenhower Dollar	N/A	$4,000	N/A	$4,000
Susan B Anthony Dollar	N/A	$1,000	N/A	$750
Sacagawea Dollar	N/A	$1,500	N/A	$1,000

Chapter 29

Wrong Planchet and Off-Metal Errors

Wrong planchet errors occur when a correctly made blank for one denomination is accidentally fed into a press for another denomination. An example would be a Jefferson Nickel struck on a Dime planchet. Wrong planchet errors have the weight of the planchet and not that specified for the coin whose design is depicted on both sides.

Off-metal errors are very similar to wrong planchet errors, although in this case the coin is struck on a metal not intended for the production regular-issue coinage. An example is a Statehood Quarter struck on an experimental planchet.

One special type of wrong planchet error is a coin struck on a planchet from a previous or later year's production involving a change in metallic composition. Wrong planchet errors of this type are known as transitional errors, the most famous of which is the 1943 "Copper" Cent struck on a bronze planchet leftover from Cent production in 1942. Normal 1943 Cents are struck zinc-plated steel because of a shortage of copper during World War II.

Undated Walking Liberty Half Dollar

Struck on a Steel Cent Planchet—PCGS MS-64

This Walking Liberty Half Dollar is struck on a planchet intended for a 1943 Steel Cent. The planchet was almost perfectly centered in the press, and the error exhibits sharp definition to the center of Liberty's portrait on the obverse and the reverse eagle.

Wrong planchet errors involving Walking Liberty Half Dollar dies are extremely rare irrespective of the planchet on which the error is struck. Approximately five examples are known that are struck on Quarter planchets, but examples struck on smaller-denomination planchets such as those intended for Cents and Nickels exist is far fewer numbers.

Ex: Fred Weinberg.

Rarity: Unique
Value: $200,000

2.

1920 Standing Liberty Quarter
Struck on a Peru, 20 Centavos Planchet—NGC MS-60 Full Head

24 millimeters. 6.9 grams. The United States Mint in Philadelphia, Pennsylvania struck copper-nickel 20 Centavos for Peru from 1918 through 1926, coins of this type bearing the attribution KM-215.1. Obviously, this planchet was intended for the issue from 1918, 1919 or 1920. Instead, it was mixed into a batch of 90% silver planchets and struck by 1920 Standing Liberty Quarter dies.

Wrong planchet errors in the Standing Liberty Quarter series are extremely rare with only a few pieces known. The coin pictured here is the only example of this type struck on a foreign planchet. It was discovered in the early 21st century and, until that point in time, was unknown in the wider numismatic market.

Rarity: Unique
Value: $75,000

3.

Undated San Francisco Mint Buffalo Nickel
Struck on a Dime Planchet—PCGS AU-58

This Buffalo Nickel was inadvertently struck on a 90% silver planchet intended for either a Barber Dime or a Mercury Dime. It is nicely positioned with most of the Native American's portrait visible on the obverse and more than half of the bison evident on the reverse. Additionally, the reverse also displays full detail to the denomination FIVE CENTS and the S mintmark.

Rarity: Unique
Value: $50,000

4.

Undated Indian Cent
Uniface Reverse Strike on a Half Dime Planchet—PCGS MS-63

A Half Dime planchet was positioned in the collar over an Indian Cent reverse die with a Cent planchet on top. The resulting impression from the dies created this dramatic error. Although the Half Dime planchet is smaller than the Indian Cent dies, virtually the entire reverse design is present.

This coin is the only Indian Cent error struck on a Half Dime planchet known from the entire series. (There is, however, an 1859 Indian Cent overstruck on a Seated Half Dime.) It had to be produced prior to 1874 since the Mint did not strike any more Half Dimes after Congress abolished that denomination through the Act of February 21, 1873.

Rarity: Unique
Value: $50,000

5.

1948 Franklin Half Dollar
Overstruck on a 1948 Lincoln Cent—NGC MS-64 Brown

Although the date of the Franklin Half Dollar is not fully discernible, I believe that this piece dates to 1948 since it is overstruck on a 1948 Lincoln Cent. In fact, considerable remnants of Lincoln's portrait are also discernible on the obverse, and portions of the wheat ears are also evident on the reverse. Both sides exhibit attractive, original toning.

This coin is one of only four Franklin Half Dollar double denomination errors known. Two of the other examples are overstruck on Quarters while the third piece is also overstruck on a Cent.

Rarity: 4 Known
Value: $50,000

6.

Undated Walking Liberty Half Dollar
Struck on a Quarter Planchet—PCGS MS-63

Fully Choice in quality, this piece also possesses razor-sharp definition to all design elements that are present on the planchet.

Rarity: 6-8 Known
Value: $50,000

7.

1942 Walking Liberty Half Dollar
Struck on a Quarter Planchet—PCGS MS-65

This 1942 Walking Liberty Half Dollar is struck on a 90% silver Quarter planchet. Both the obverse and reverse impressions are rather well centered in the context of the error, and the date is discernible (although not full) at the lower-obverse border.

Long-regarded as classics in the family of major U.S. Mint error, wrong planchet Walking Liberty Half Dollars are eagerly sought by both specialized errors collectors and numismatists that are assembling advanced collections of this popular 20th century silver type.

Rarity: 6-8 Known
Value: $50,000

8.

1944 Walking Liberty Half Dollar
Struck on a Quarter Planchet—PCGS MS-65

The strike is nicely centered on the planchet with only the outmost elements of the peripheral devices absent. Enough of the date is discernible to attribute this coin to 1944.

Ex: Rare Coins from the Abe Kosoff Estate (Bowers and Merena, 11/1985), lot 4187.

Rarity: 6-8 Known
Value: $50,000

9.

1869 Indian Cent
Struck on a Dime Planchet—PCGS AU-55

This wrong planchet error from the Indian Cent series is struck on a silver planchet intended for use in the Seated Dime series.

The early years of this coin's pedigree are quite impressive:

Ex: Woodin Collection of Patterns, Die Trials and Mint Errors (1913); plate coin in the 1913 book United States Pattern Trial, and Experimental Pieces by Edgar H. Adams and William H. Woodin; Brenner; exhibited at the American Numismatic Society (ANS) in 1914.

The coin has also listed (as an error) in the book *United States Pattern, Experimental and Trial Pieces* by Dr. J. Hewitt Judd.

Rarity: 3 Known
Value: $50,000

10.

1945 Walking Liberty Half Dollar
Struck on an El Salvador, 25 Centavo Planchet—NGC MS-63

El Salvador 25 Centavos of the KM-136 type were struck in the United States Mint during 1943 and 1944. Apparently, a planchet from those issues remained on hand in 1945 and subsequently found its way into a press that was striking 1945 Walking Liberty Half Dollars. The El Salvador planchet is considerably thinner and lighter than that of the Walking Liberty Half Dollar, and it is nearly the same thickness of a U.S. Dime. Since there was not enough metal to fill the deepest recesses of the dies, this piece exhibits noticeably blunt definition over the central highpoints of the Walking Liberty design.

There are only two wrong planchet Walking Liberty Half Dollar errors known that involve a foreign planchet. This particular example is the only one struck on an El Salvador 25 Centavos planchet.

Rarity: Unique
Value: $40,000

11.

1909 Indian Cent
Struck on a Dime Planchet—PCGS AU-58

This final-year Indian Cent is struck on a 90% silver planchet intended for a Barber Dime. The Dime planchet is slightly smaller than the Cent dies (17.9 millimeters vs. 19 millimeters), with the result that this error is a bit softly defined around the periphery and in a few isolated areas toward the centers. There was not enough metal in the planchet to completely fill the dies. On the other hand, this piece retains nearly full mint luster.

Rarity: 2 Known
Value: $40,000

12.

1882 Shield Nickel
Struck on a Cent Planchet—NGC MS-65 Brown

A wrong planchet error from the second-to-last year of the Shield Nickel series, this 1882 is struck on a bronze planchet that the Mint intended to use in the production of Indian Cents. A few peripheral devices are slightly off the planchet, but the definition is otherwise sharp.

The Shield Nickel series of 1866-1883 has yielded very few major mint errors, a fact that confirms the significance of this fully original Gem.

Rarity: 5 Known
Value: $40,000

13.

1873 Open 3 Shield Nickel
Struck on a Cent Planchet—PCGS MS-62

Another rare and important Mint error from the Shield Nickel series, this 1873 Open 3 is struck on a bronze Indian Cent planchet.

Ex: King Farouk of Egypt; Palace Collection (Sotheby's, 2/1954), part of lot 1924; Fred Weinberg. The Sotheby's cataloger seems to have mistaken this error for a bronze die trial striking of the 1873 Shield Nickel on a small planchet since the coin was sold in a lot of 1873-dated pattern coinage.

Rarity: 5 Known
Value: $40,000

14.

1871 Three-Cent Nickel
Struck on a Cent Stock—NGC MS-62 Brown

This planchet should have been prepared for use in a press that was striking Indian Cents. Instead, it was punched in the diameter of a Three-Cent Nickel (17.9 millimeters) and subsequently used to produce a coin of that type.

This coin is the only wrong planchet error attributed to the Three-Cent Nickel series of 1865-1889.

Rarity: Unique
Value: $35,000

15.

1866 Rays Shield Nickel
Struck on a Cent Planchet—PCGS EF-45

The Mint should have used this planchet to produce a bronze Indian Cent. Instead, it was fed into the wrong press and was struck by dies for the 1866 Rays Shield Nickel.

This is one of the most important Shield Nickel errors known. It was struck during the first year that the United States Mint produced Nickel Five-Cent pieces. Even more significantly, it is an example of the Rays design that the Mint used only in 1866 and 1867. There are only two other wrong planchet errors known that involve the Rays Shield Nickel type.

Rarity: 3 Known
Value: $35,000

16.

1864 Large Motto Two-Cent Piece
Struck on a Cent Planchet—NGC AU-58 Brown

The strike on this extremely rare two-cent piece is well centered, although the smaller size of the Cent planchet relative to the Two-Cent dies has resulted in some of the peripheral devices being partially off the planchet. Enough of the date is discernible, however, that I can attribute this important piece to the first year of the Two-Cent series.

Rarity: 4 Known
Value: $30,000

17.

Undated Eisenhower Dollar
Struck on a Cent Planchet—PCGS MS-64 Brown

One of the ultimate Eisenhower Dollars available in today's market, this piece is struck on a bronze planchet intended for an Indian Cent. Much of Eisenhower's portrait is visible on the obverse, while the reverse reveals more than half of the eagle.

Ex: Private Mint Error Collection (formed in the 1970s).

Rarity: 5 Known
Value: $25,000

18.

1876 Indian Cent
Struck on a Three-Cent Nickel Planchet—NGC MS-64

The coin has also listed (as an error) in the book *United States Pattern, Experimental and Trial Pieces* by Dr. J. Hewitt Judd and on the website www.uspatterns.com.

This error Indian Cent is struck on a copper-nickel planchet that weighs 1.68 grams. This weight is within the legal tolerance of +/- 0.26 grams for a 1.94-gram weight standard. The only copper-nickel planchets produced to this weight standard that were in use in the Philadelphia Mint in 1876 were those intended for the Three-Cent Nickel series. Both sides of this coin are sharply struck with reflective, semi-prooflike fields.

Not only are wrong planchet errors from the Indian Cent series very rare coins, but the present example has the added distinction of being an example of a scarcer, semi key-date issue from the 1870s.

Rarity: 3 Known
Value: $25,000

19.

Undated Eisenhower Dollar
Struck on a Copper-Nickel Clad Planchet—PCGS MS-63

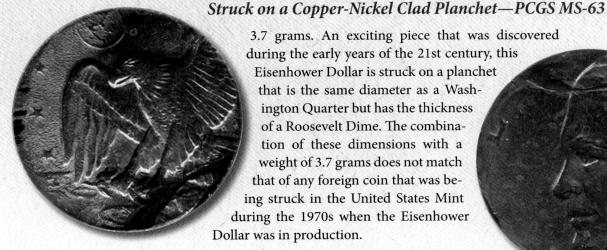

3.7 grams. An exciting piece that was discovered during the early years of the 21st century, this Eisenhower Dollar is struck on a planchet that is the same diameter as a Washington Quarter but has the thickness of a Roosevelt Dime. The combination of these dimensions with a weight of 3.7 grams does not match that of any foreign coin that was being struck in the United States Mint during the 1970s when the Eisenhower Dollar was in production.

Rarity: Unique
Value: $15,000

20.

1944 Washington Quarter

Struck on a Nickel Planchet—NGC MS-62

An early-date error from the Washington Quarter series, this piece is struck on a Wartime Jefferson Nickel planchet with a composition of 56% copper, 35% silver and 9% manganese.

The brevity of the Wartime Jefferson Nickel series (four years from 1942 through 1945) explains the extreme rarity of wrong planchet errors involving this alloy.

Rarity: 3 Known
Value: $10,000

21.

Undated Denver Mint Franklin Half Dollar

Struck on a Cent Planchet—NGC MS-66 Brown

Franklin Half Dollars struck on smaller planchets intended for Cents, Nickels and Dimes are very scarce. When they are offered in today's market, such pieces usually grade EF or AU. As a premium-quality Gem, the example pictured here is among the finest known for this dramatic error type.

Rarity: 20 Known
Value: $7,500

22.

1944 Lincoln Cent
Struck on a Dime Planchet—PCGS EF-40

This 1944 Cent is struck on a 90% silver planchet intended for a Mercury Dime.

Unlike the 1943 "Silver" Cents, of which approximately 25 pieces are known, the 1944 "Silver" Cent is a major numismatic rarity with just four examples believed to exist.

Rarity: 4 Known
Value: $5,000

23.

SMS 1965 Washington Quarter
Struck on a Nickel Planchet—ANACS MS-63

The planchet expanded in an attempt to fill the much larger Quarter dies, and the error actually features virtually complete definition to both sides. The date is full, and only the tops of the letters ERTY in the word LIBERTY on the obverse and the bottoms of the letters in the denomination QUARTER DOLLAR on the reverse are off the planchet.

Special Mint Set (SMS) errors are even rarer than proof errors, a fact that we can contribute to the brevity of the Mint's usage of the SMS finish. Regular-issue coins struck with that finish were produced only in 1965, 1966 and 1967.

Rarity: Unique
Value: $5,000

Price Guide for Wrong Planchet and Off-Metal Errors

Denomination	Off-Metal Planchet	Circulated	AU	Unc	Choice Unc – Gem
Indian Cent	Foreign Planchet	$1,000	$1,500	$5,000	$7,500
Indian Cent	Dime Planchet	$20,000	$30,000	$50,000	$75,000
Lincoln Cent Before 1919	Dime Planchet	$4,000	$6,500	$10,000	–
Lincoln Cent Before 1919	Foreign Planchet	$750	$2,000	$4,000	–
Lincoln Cent 1919–1940	Dime Planchet	$2,000	$2,500	$4,000	$6,000
Lincoln Cent 1919–1940	Foreign Planchet	$500	$1,000	$1,500	$2,500
Lincoln Cent 1943 Steel	Dime Planchet	$1,500	$2,500	$3,500	$7,500
Lincoln Cent 1943 Transitional	Copper Cent Planchet	$75,000	$100,000	$150,000	$200,000
Lincoln Cent 1944 Transitional	Steel Cent Planchet	$30,000	$50,000	$100,000	$150,000
Lincoln Cent Wheat Ears (1941–1964)	Dime Planchet	$500	$600	$1,000	$2,000
Lincoln Cent 1965 and Later	Dime Planchet	$125	$150	$200	$350
Lincoln Cent 1964 Transitional	Clad Dime Planchet	$2,500	$4,000	$7,500	$10,000
Lincoln Cent 1965 Transitional	Silver Dime Planchet	$2,750	$4,500	$6,000	$7,500
Shield Nickel	Foreign Planchet	$7,500	$12,500	–	–
Shield Nickel	Cent Planchet	$15,000	$25,000	$40,000	$60,000
Liberty Nickel	Foreign Planchet	$400	$750	$1,250	$2,000
Liberty Nickel	Cent Planchet	$2,000	$3,000	$6,000	$7,500
Buffalo Nickel	Foreign Planchet	$2,500	$7,500	$12,500	–
Buffalo Nickel	Cent Planchet	$2,000	$4,000	$6,000	$8,000
Jefferson Nickel Before 1950	Cent Planchet	$250	$500	$750	$1,000
Jefferson Nickel 1950 and Later	Cent Planchet	$125	$150	$200	$250
Jefferson Nickel 1943	Steel Cent Planchet	$1,000	$2,000	$3,000	$5,000
Jefferson Nickel 1964 and Earlier	Silver Dime Planchet	$200	$300	$350	$400
Jefferson Nickel 1965 and Later	Clad Dime Planchet	$150	$200	$225	$250
Roosevelt Dime Silver	Foreign Planchet	$2,000	$2,500	$3,000	$3,500
Roosevelt Dime Clad	Foreign Planchet	$1,500	$2,000	$2,250	$2,500
Roosevelt Dime 1964 Transitional	Clad Dime Planchet	$5,000	$6,500	$10,000	$12,500
Roosevelt Dime 1965 Transitional	Silver Dime Planchet	$5,000	$6,500	$7,500	$8,500
Washington Quarter Silver	Cent Planchet	$300	$400	$500	$750
Washington Quarter Silver	Nickel Planchet	$300	$400	$500	$600
Washington Quarter Clad	Cent Planchet	$250	$300	$400	$500
Washington Quarter Clad	Nickel Planchet	$100	$150	$200	$250
Washington Quarter	Silver Dime Planchet	$300	$400	$500	$650
Washington Quarter	Clad Dime Planchet	$250	$300	$350	$400
Washington Quarter 1964 Transitional	Clad Quarter Planchet	$5,000	$6,500	$7,500	$12,500
Washington Quarter 1965 Transitional	Silver Quarter Planchet	$5,000	$6,500	$7,500	$8,500

Price Guide for Wrong Planchet and Off-Metal Errors (continued)

Denomination	Off-Metal Planchet	Circulated	AU	Unc	Choice Unc – Gem
Delaware State Quarter	Nickel Planchet	N/A	$500	$650	$750
All Other State Quarters	Nickel Planchet	N/A	$1,000	$1,250	$1,500
State Quarter	Dime Planchet	N/A	$5,000	$5,500	$6,000
Walking Half	Quarter Planchet	$17,500	$22,500	$40,000	$50,000
Walking Half	Foreign Planchet	$10,000	$15,000	$30,000	$40,000
Franklin Half	Cent Planchet	$3,000	$4,000	$5,000	$6,000
Franklin Half	Nickel Planchet	$3,000	$4,000	$5,000	$6,000
Franklin Half	Dime Planchet	$3,500	$4,500	$5,500	$6,500
Franklin Half	Quarter Planchet	$600	$750	$1,000	$1,250
Kennedy Half Silver 1964	Cent Planchet	$1,000	$1,250	$1,500	$2,000
Kennedy Half Silver 1964	Nickel Planchet	$1,000	$1,250	$1,500	$2,000
Kennedy Half Silver 1964	Dime Planchet	$1,000	$1,250	$2,000	$2,500
Kennedy Half Silver 1964	Quarter Planchet	$400	$500	$600	$750
Kennedy Half Clad	Cent Planchet	$750	$850	$1,000	$1,500
Kennedy Half Clad	Nickel Planchet	$750	$850	$1,000	$1,250
Kennedy Half Clad	Dime Planchet	$750	$850	$1,000	$1,400
Kennedy Half Clad	Quarter Planchet	$350	$400	$450	$500
Kennedy Half 1964 Transitional	Clad Half Planchet	$5,000	$6,000	$10,000	$12,500
Kennedy Half 1965 Transitional	Silver Half Planchet	$5,000	$6,500	$7,500	$10,000
Kennedy Half 1964 Transitional	Clad Quarter Planchet	$5,000	$7,500	$10,000	$12,500
Kennedy Half 1965 Transitional	Silver Quarter Planchet	$6,000	$7,500	$8,000	$9,000
Eisenhower Dollar	Cent Planchet	$10,000	$12,500	$15,000	$20,000
Eisenhower Dollar	Nickel Planchet	$10,000	$12,500	$15,000	$20,000
Eisenhower Dollar	Dime Planchet	$7,500	$8,500	$15,000	$20,000
Eisenhower Dollar	Quarter Planchet	$10,000	$12,500	$15,000	$20,000
Eisenhower Dollar	Half Planchet	$1,600	$1,750	$2,000	$3,000
Eisenhower Dollar	Foreign Planchet	$900	$1,000	$1,250	$1,500
Eisenhower Dollar Transitional	40% Silver Planchet	$2,750	$3,000	$3,500	$5,000
Susan B Anthony Dollar	Cent Planchet	N/A	$1,750	$3,000	$5,000
Susan B Anthony Dollar	Nickel Planchet	N/A	$6,000	$7,000	$8,000
Susan B Anthony Dollar	Dime Planchet	N/A	$6,000	$7,000	$10,000
Susan B Anthony Dollar	Quarter Planchet	N/A	$600	$850	$1,000
Sacagawea Dollar	Cent Planchet	N/A	$12,500	$15,000	$20,000
Sacagawea Dollar	Nickel Planchet	N/A	$12,500	$15,000	$20,000
Sacagawea Dollar	Dime Planchet	N/A	$8,000	$15,000	$20,000
Sacagawea Dollar	Quarter Planchet	N/A	$1,500	$2,000	$2,500

*I*n 2007, the U.S. Mint began striking a new series of Dollar coins to commemorate the presidents of the United States. These coins feature a lettered edge that includes the date, mintmark and the mottoes IN GOD WE TRUST and E PLURIBUS UNUM. They are the first U.S. coins produced with lettered edges since the end of the Indian Eagle and Saint-Gaudens Double Eagle series in 1933.

The introduction of this series has allowed the discovery of a new type of error on U.S. coins. Some of the Presidential Dollars inadvertently left the Mint without the edge lettering. Since the mintmark position is on the edge, it is normally impossible to tell whether the error in question is attributable to the Philadelphia or Denver Mint. Missing edge lettering errors on 2007 George Washington Presidential Dollars, however, are attributable to issuing Mint by still looking at the edges. Those pieces struck in the Denver Mint have no copper core visible because they were rinsed in a solution that coated the edge. The copper core is visible on the edge of Philadelphia Mint examples.

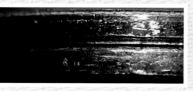

1.

Undated (2007-P) George Washington Presidential Dollar

Missing Edge Lettering—NGC MS-65

The date and mintmark are absent from this Presidential Dollar since the edge is blank. The use of the George Washington obverse design, however, dates this piece to 2007—the first year of the Presidential Dollar series.

This coin is encapsulated in an NGC holder that has been signed by Director of the United States Mint Edmund C. Moy. Moy hosted a collector forum at the 2007 American Numismatic Association (ANA) National Money Show in Charlotte, North Carolina. He was also available to the public from 11 o'clock A.M. to noon on March 16 at the Mint's booth on the show bourse.

2.

Undated (2007-P) George Washington Presidential Dollar

Missing Edge Lettering and Clad Layer— NGC MS-65

A double error, this piece is missing not only the edge lettering, but also the reverse clad layer. This is the only error of this kind of which I am aware of on the Washington Presidential Dollar.

3.

Undated (2007) John Adams Presidential Dollar

Missing Edge Lettering—PCGS MS-65

Once again, the obverse portrait dates this Presidential Dollar to 2007.

The John Adams type is the second issue in the Presidential Dollar series, and it is much more challenging to locate as a Missing Edge Letter error than the George Washington type.

4.

Undated (2007) Thomas Jefferson Presidential Dollar

Missing Edge Lettering—PCGS MS-68

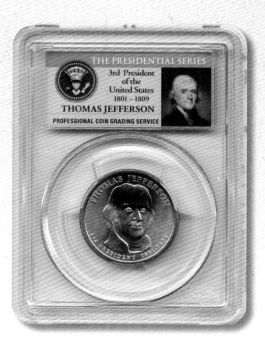

Only a few hundred Thomas Jefferson Dollars are known with no lettering on the edge. By comparison, the George Washington Presidential Dollar type has yielded thousands of such errors.

Price Guide for Missing Edge Lettering

Prices as of September 20, 2008 and are for certified coins by PCGS or NGC

Denomination	Quantity	MS 63	MS 64	MS 65	MS 66	MS 67
Washington (Uncirculated)	est 100,000 - 150,000	$80	$135	$185	$300	$2,500
Washington (Satin Finish)	1 Known	--	--	--	$10,000	--
Adams (Uncirculated)	est 10,000 - 12,000	$400	$550	$750	$1,500	$3,500
Adams (Satin Finish)	125 Known	$4,000	$6,000	$7,000	$9,000	$13,000
Jefferson (Uncirculated)	est 850 - 1,000	$2,000	$2,500	$4,000	$6,000	$8,000
Jefferson (Satin Finish)	250 Reported	$2,500	$3,000	$4,500	$6,500	$9,000
Madison (Uncirculated)	7 Known	--	--	--	--	--
Madison (Satin Finish)	Several dozen Reported	--	--	--	--	--
Monroe (Uncirculated)	Unknown	--	--	--	--	--
Monroe (Satin Finish)	2 Certified at PCGS 3 Reported in *Coin World*	--	--	--	--	--
John Q Adams (Uncirculated)	Unknown	--	--	--	--	--
John Q Adams (Satin Finish)	Unknown	--	--	--	--	--
Jackson (Uncirculated)	Unknown	--	--	--	--	--
Jackson (Satin Finish)	3 Reported in *Coin World*	--	--	--	--	--

U.S. Coin Weights and Specifications

Denomination	Issue Date	W./Grs	Tolerance in Grains	Die (mm)	Thick (mm)	S.G.	Composition
Half Cent	1793-1795	104		23.5		8.92	Pure Copper
	1796-1857	84		23.5		8.92	Pure Copper
Large Cent	1793-1795	208		26-28		8.92	Pure Copper
	1796-1857	168		29		8.92	Pure Copper
Small Cent	1856-1864	72	2	19.3	2.2	8.92	88 Cu, 12 Ni
	1864-1942	48	2	19.05	2.2	8.84	95 Cu, 5 tin/zinc
	1943	42.5	2	19.05	1.575	7.8	Zinc coated steel
	1944-1946	48	2	19.05	1.575	8.86	70 Cu, 30 zinc
	1947-1962	48	2	19.05	1.575	8.84	95 Cu, 5 tin/zinc
	1963-1982	48	2	19.05	1.575	8.86	95 Cu, 5 zinc
	1982-Date	38.58		19.05	1.575	7.17	Copper Plated Zinc
Two Cent	1864-1873	96		23		8.84	Cu, 5 tin/zinc
3¢ Nickel	1865-1889	30		17.9		8.92	75 Cu, 25 Ni
3¢ Silver	1851-1853	12.375		14		10.11	75 Ag, 25 Cu
	1854-1873	11.52		14		10.34	90 Ag, 10 Cu
Five Cent	1866-1883	77.16	3	20.5	1.981	8.92	75 Cu, 25 Ni
	1883-1942	77.16		21.21	1.989	8.92	75 Cu, 25 Ni
	1942-1945	77.16	3	21.21	1.981	9.32	35 Ag, 56 Cu, 9 Mg
	1946-Date	77.16	3	21.21	1.981	8.92	74 Cu, 25 Ni
Half Dime	1794-1805	20.8		16.5	.7	10.32	90 Ag, 10 Cu
	1829-1837	20.8		15.5		10.32	90 Ag, 10 Cu
	1829-1837 ?	20		15.5		10.34	90 Ag, 10 Cu
	1853-1873	19.2		15.5		10.34	90 Ag, 10 Cu
Dime	1796-1828	41.6		18.8		10.32	89.2 Ag, 10.8 Cu
	1828-1837	41.6		17.9		10.32	90 Ag, 10 Cu
	1837-1853	41.25	1.5	17.9	1.346	10.34	90 Ag, 10 Cu
	1853-1873	38.4	1.5	17.9	1.346	10.34	90 Ag, 10 Cu
	1873-1964	38.58	1.5	17.9		10.34	90 Ag, 10 Cu
	1965-Date	35		17.9		8.92	75 Cu, 25 Ni on Cu core
Twenty Cent	1875-1878	77.16		22.5		10.34	90 Ag, 10 Cu
Quarter	1796-1828	104		27		10.32	89 Ag, 11 Cu
	1831-1839	104		24.3			90 Ag, 10 Cu
	1837-1853	103.12	3	24.26		10.34	90 Ag, 10 Cu
	1853-1873	96	3	24.26		10.34	90 Ag, 10 Cu
	1873-1964	96.45	3	24.26	1.701	10.34	90 Ag, 10 Cu
	1965-Date	87.5	3	24.26	1.701	8.95	75 Cu, 25 Ni on Cu
	1976 (40%)	88.74	3	24.26		9.53	80 Cu, 20 Ag on 20 Ag, 80 Cu core

Denomination	Issue Date	W./Grs	Tolerance in Grains	Die (mm)	Thick (mm)	S.G.	Composition
Half Dollar	1794-1836	208		32.5	1.75	10.32	89 Ag, 11 Cu
	1836-1853	206.25	4	30.6	1.75	10.34	90 Ag, 10 Cu
	1853-1873	192	4	30.6	1.75	10.34	90 Ag, 10 Cu
	1873-1964	192.9	4	30.6	2.184	10.34	90 Ag, 10 Cu
	1965-1970	177.5	4	30.6	2.184	9.53	80 Ag, 20 Cu, 20 Ag core
	1971-Date	175		30.6	2.184	8.92	75 Cu, 25 Ni on Cu
	1976 (40%)	177.47	6	30.6		9.53	80 Ag, 20 Cu on 20 Ag, 80 Cu core
Silver Dollar	1794-1803	416	39-40	10.32			89 Ag, 11 Cu
	1840-1935	412	6	38.1	2.896	10.34	90 Ag, 10 Cu
Eisenhower $1-Clad	1971-1978	350	38.1	8.92			75 Cu, 25 Ni on Cu core
Eisenhower $1-Silver	1971-1976	379.5	38.1	9.53			80 Ag, 20 Cu on 20 Ag, 80 Cu core
Trade Dollar	1873-1885	420	38.1	10.34			90 Ag, 10 Cu
Susan B Anthony Dollar	1979-1981	125	6	26.5		8.92	75 Cu, 25 Ni on Cu core
Commemorative Dollar	1983-1988	412.5		38.1		10.34	
American Eagle $1	1986-Date	479.9		40.6			99.93 Ag, .07 Cu
Susan B Anthony Dollar	1999						
Sacagawea $1	2000						
Gold Dollar T-1	1849-1854	25.8	0.25	13		17.16	900 Au, 100 Cu
T-2	1854-1856	25.8	0.25	14.86		17.16	900 Au, 100 Cu
T-3	1856-1889	25.8	0.25	14.86		17.16	900 Au, 100 Cu
$2.5 Gold	1796-1808	67.5	0.25	20		17.45	917 Au, 83 Cu
	1821-1827	67.5	0.25	18.5		17.14	917 Au, 83 Cu
	1829-1834	67.5		18.2		17.45	917 Au, 83 Cu
	1834-1839	64.5	18.2	17.14			900 Au, 100 Cu
	1840-1929	64.5	.25	18		17.16	900 Au, 100 Cu
$3 Gold	1854-1889	77.4	.25	20.63		17.16	900 Au, 100 Cu
$5 Gold	1795-1829	135	.25	25		17.45	916 Au, 84 Cu
	1829-1834	135		22.5		17.45	916 Au, 84 Cu
	1834-1838	129	.25	22.5		17.14	899 Au, 101 Cu
	1839-1840	129	22.5	17.16			900 Au, 100 Cu
	1840-1929	129	.25	21.6		17.16	900 Au, 100 Cu
Commemorative Gold	1986-Date	129		21.6		17.6	
American Eagle $5	1986-Date	52.35		16.5			91.67 Au, 390 Ag, 5.3390 Cu
$10 Gold	1795-1804	270	.5	33	33	17.45	917 Au, 83 Cu
	1838-1933	258	.5	27	17.16		900 Au, 100 Cu
Olympic	1984	258		27			900 Au, 100 Cu
American Eagle $10	1986-Date	130.9		22			91.67 Au, 390 Ag, 5.3390 Cu
$20 Gold	1850-1933	516	.5	34	2.6	17.16	900 Au, 100 Cu
American Eagle $25	1986-Date	261.8		27			91.67 Au, 390 Ag, 5.3390 Cu
American Eagle $50	1986-Date	523.6		32.7			

The Minting Process

The following photographs were taken by a group of error coin dealers on a tour of the Philadelphia Mint's facilities. They illustrate different stages of the minting process during which major mint errors can occur.

Figure 1: These rolled strips will eventually be punched into blank planchets for Quarters.

Figure 2: Cent planchets being fed into the feeder mechanism prior to striking.

NOTICE

The red tanks marked **SWEEPS** are to be used as the receptacles for mixed blanks/coins swept off the floor when sweeping

MAXIMUM CIRCULATING COINAGE DIE TONNAGES		
(Safety Limits)		
DENOM	NORMAL WORKING	MAXIMUM
1¢	35 T	60 T
5¢	50 T	75 T
10¢	35 T	50 T
25¢	60 T	95 T
50¢	120 T	150 T
$1.00	85 T	115 T

Figure 3: The new Schuler presses used in the United States Mint have virtually eliminated mint errors.

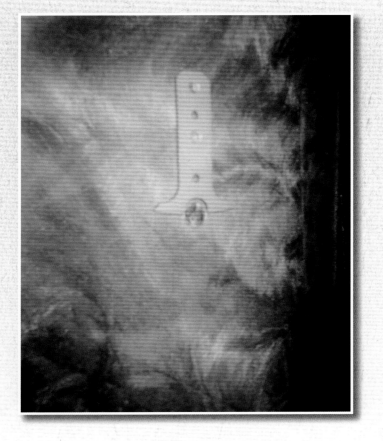

Figure 4: A feeder finger that the Mint uses in the production of coins. Many denominations of U.S. coins have been struck on the tips of feeder fingers. Even so, this is an extremely rare mint error.

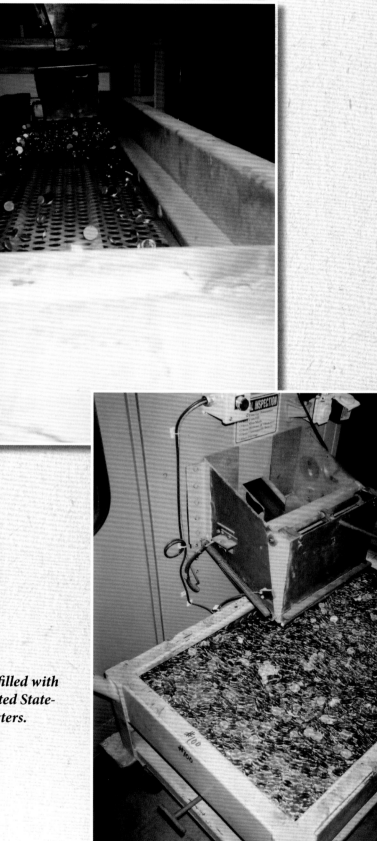

Figure 5: After striking, coins are passed across a riddler machine whose bouncing mechanism is designed to filter out mint errors.

Figure 6: A tote bin filled with newly minted Statehood Quarters.

225

Figure 7: This picture of a tote bin clearly shows a few leftover blank planchets trapped at the bottom near the "trap door." If this tote bin were used in the production of coins of a different denomination without being thoroughly inspected by Mint personnel, the leftover planchets could be struck into wrong planchet errors.

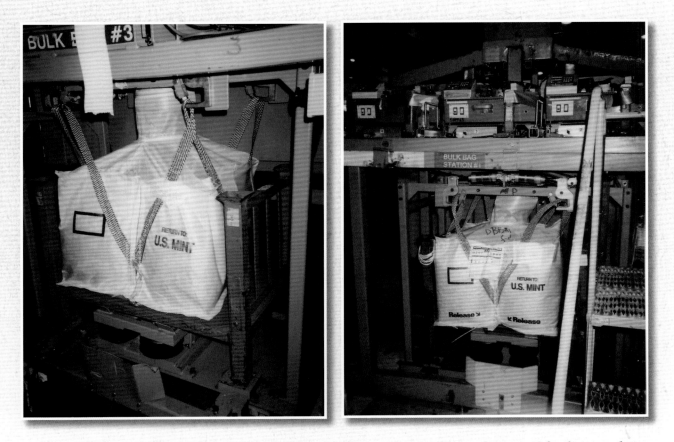

Figure 8: These two photos illustrate the ballistic bag operation. These bags are sent to facilities such as banks that distribute coins into circulation.

Historic Price Appreciation
for Select Mint Errors

From 1975 through 1978, I mailed out more than 25 fixed price lists of major mint errors. When I look back at these price lists, I am amazed at how inexpensive these coins were in the mid-1970s compared to the value in the numismatic market of the early 21st century. In order to provide you with a sense of how much the error coin market has grown during this time period, I have provided a brief list of coins taken from my first fixed price list, the prices that they were offered at in 1975 and their value in the 2009 market.

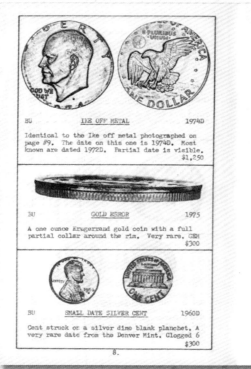

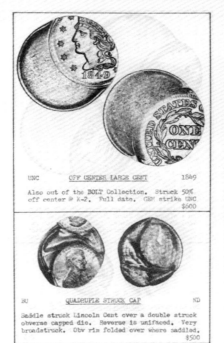

1849 Coronet Cent—

Struck 50% Off Center
1975 Value: $600
2009 Value: $15,000

1899 Indian Cent—

Overstruck on an 1899 Barber Dime
  1975 Value: $1,750
  2009 Value: $40,000

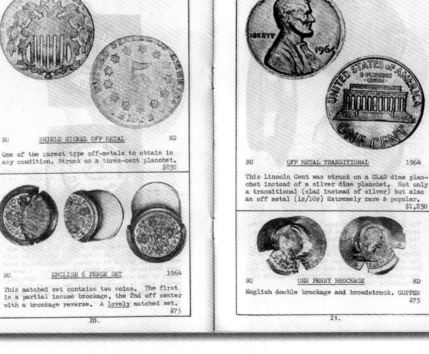

1909 Indian Cent—

Struck on a Quarter Eagle Planchet
  1975 Value: $20,000
  2009 Value: $150,000

Undated No Rays Shield Nickel—

Struck on a Three-Cent Nickel Planchet
  1975 Value: $850
  2009 Value: $25,000

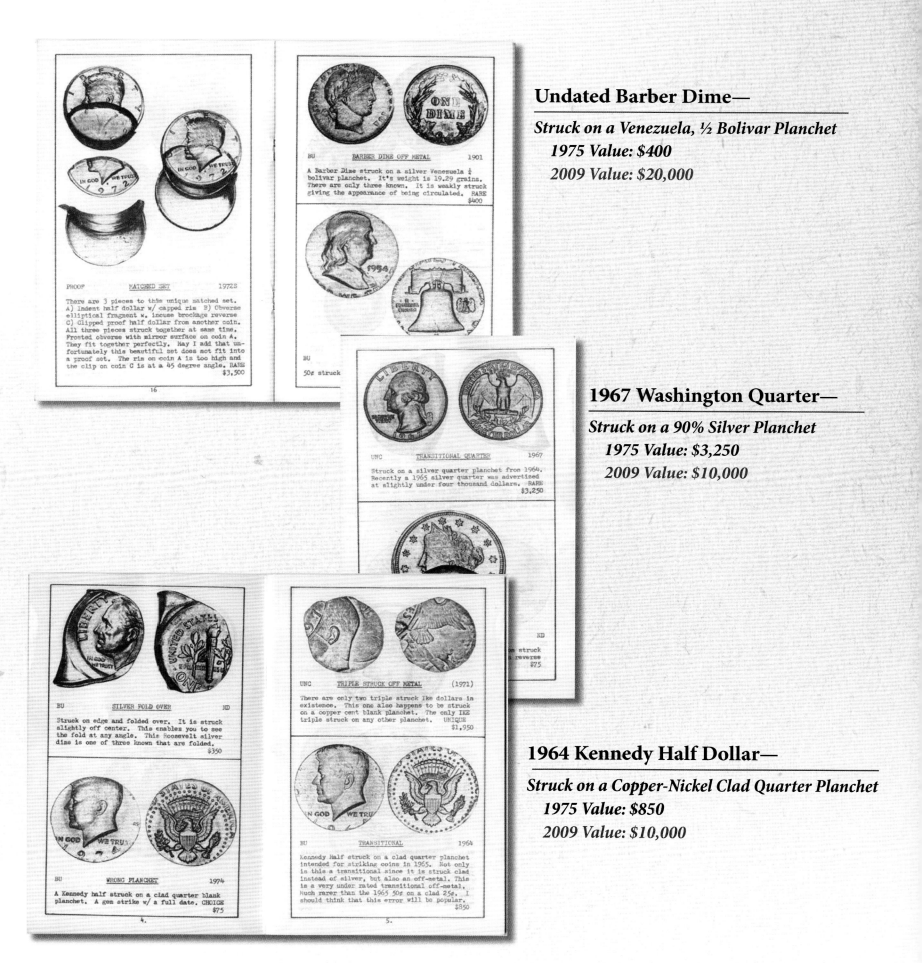

Undated Barber Dime—

Struck on a Venezuela, ½ Bolivar Planchet
1975 Value: $400
2009 Value: $20,000

1967 Washington Quarter—

Struck on a 90% Silver Planchet
1975 Value: $3,250
2009 Value: $10,000

1964 Kennedy Half Dollar—

Struck on a Copper-Nickel Clad Quarter Planchet
1975 Value: $850
2009 Value: $10,000

229

Undated Eisenhower Dollar—

Triple Struck on a Cent Planchet
1975 Value: $1,950
2009 Value: $30,000

1851 Liberty Double Eagle—

Struck on a Large Cent Planchet
1975 Value: $12,500
2009 Value: $150,000

Bibliography

Altz, Charles G. and Barton, E.H. *Foreign Coins Struck at the United States Mints*. Racine, Wisconsin: Whitman Publishing Company, 1965.

Bowers, Q. David. *Silver Dollars & Trade Dollars of the United States: A Complete Encyclopedia, Volume One*. Wolfeboro, New Hampshire: Bowers and Merena Galleries, Inc., 1993.

Browning, A.W. *The Early Quarter Dollars of the United States: 1796-1838*. Wolfeboro, New Hampshire: Bowers and Merena Galleries, Inc., 1992.

Bruce, Colin R., II, Ed. *2008 Standard Catalog of World Coins: 1901-2000, 35th Official Edition*. Iola, Wisconsin: Krause Publications, 2007.

Bruce, Colin R., II, Ed. *Standard Catalog of World Coins: 1801-1900, 5th Official Edition*. Iola, Wisconsin: Krause Publications, 2006.

Cline, J.H. *Standing Liberty Quarters, Fourth Edition*. Irvine, California: Zyrus Press, 2007.

Dannreuther, John W. and Bass, Harry W., Jr. *Early U.S. Gold Coin Varieties: A Study of Die States, 1795-1834*. Atlanta, Georgia: Whitman Publishing, LLC, 2006.

Davenport, John S. *European Crowns and Talers since 1800, Second Edition*. London, England: Spink and Son, Ltd., 1964.

Fivaz, Bill and Stanton, J.T. *Cherrypickers' Guide to Rare Die Varieties of United States Coins, Fourth Edition, Volume II*. Atlanta, Georgia: Whitman Publishing, LLC, 2006.

Friedberg, Arthur L. and Friedberg, Ira S. *Gold Coins of the World: From Ancient Times to the Present, 7th Edition*. Clifton, New Jersey: The Coin and Currency Institute, Inc., 2003.

Garrett, Jeff and Guth, Ron. *Encyclopedia of U.S. Gold Coins: 1795-1933*. Atlanta, Georgia: Whitman Publishing, LLC, 2006.

Judd, J. Hewitt, M.D. *United States Pattern Coins, Ninth Edition*. Atlanta, Georgia: Whitman Publishing, LLC, 2005.

Kagin, Donald H., Ph.D. *Private Gold Coins and Patterns of the United States*. New York, New York: Arco Publishing, Inc., 1981.

Margolis, Arnold and Weinberg, Fred. *The Error Coin Encyclopedia, Fourth Edition*. Arnold Margolis and Fred Weinberg, 2004.